D0627764

TRAUMA

TRAUMA

a collection of short stories

Elizabeth Jaikaran

Shanti Arts Publishing

Brunswick, Maine

TRAUMA

a collection of short stories

Copyright © 2017 Elizabeth Jaikaran

All rights reserved. No part of this book may be
used or reproduced in any manner whatsoever
without the written permission of the publisher.

Published by Shanti Arts Publishing
Cover and interior design by Shanti Arts Designs
Cover image by Khalidah Abubaker of Creative Differences

Shanti Arts LLC
Brunswick, Maine
www.shantiarts.com

Printed in the United States of America

First Edition

*This is a work of creative non-fiction. The characters are based
on real people and the stories are true, though some names
and identifying details have been changed to preserve the
privacy of certain persons. Relying on notes and memory, the
author has made every effort to respectfully and accurately
present the stories told to her by family members and friends.*

ISBN: 978-1-941830-42-0 (softcover)
ISBN: 978-1-941830-43-7 (digital)

LCCN: 2017942499

To my mom and dad, Jenny and Wazir,
for giving me a beautiful life.

To Professors Carol Gilligan and David Richards,
for reaffirming my purpose in writing.

And to all the women whose lives make the
pages that follow the experience that it is.
Your pains and joys are my own.

Acknowledgments

— Rajshri Productions for permission to quote from the song "Meri Dosti Mera Pyaar" from the film *Dosti*.

— Prasad Productions Pvt. Ltd. for permission to quote from the song "Usko Nahin Dekha Hamne Kabhi" from the film *Daadi Maa*.

Acknowledgments

— Kashav Productions for permission to quote from the song "Mehboob Mere" sung in a film *Philip Don*.

— Pixel Productions Pvt. Ltd. for permission to quote from the song "Hoshi Wala Kuch To Gadbad Hai" from the film *Bunty Aur...*

Contents

Contents

Introduction

As I write this introduction, trauma manifests all around me in the forms of war, heartbreak, and devastating injustice. It is a component of the human experience that endures across the expanse of time and geography. It is the one common thread of seemingly variable human life, and along with it is our ability to be deeply hurt, deeply impacted, and profoundly changed by externalities that we never thought would permeate our lives. These stories seem as poignant now as they ever did, a testament to the ever tumultuous nature of this planet: forever in imperceptible motion and collision and ruin, followed by equally imperceptible rest and rebirth and restoration.

This book began as a final paper I wrote during my third year at New York University School of Law while taking a course taught by Professors Carol Gilligan and David Richards titled "Resisting Injustice." It was a seminar in which we engaged with published narratives on resistance and discussed the impact of trauma on collective identities.

It was in this course that I began to think, specifically, of the experiences that have so impacted the women around me: from my best friend to my great-grandmothers. I reflected upon so many aspects of their experiences. How much of their pain and suffering was caused by men? How much of their pain and suffering was caused by unjust institutions? How much of their pain and suffering was caused by the judicious heavens and stars?

I reflected, gathered as much information as I could, and began to write. But not just write. I placed myself into their traumatic episodes. I closed my eyes and imagined myself being back in the old country, walking on dirt roads and eating dinner with grandparents who still spoke Hindi and Urdu, with wrists still adorned with ancestral silver from China, and were just two generations removed from the vile history of slavery. I imagined myself in villages where time passed slowly and small lizards danced around the bedroom. I imagined myself collapsing in grief, shaking in fear, and crying in defeat. I imagined myself witnessing horrors that I knew I would not survive if I actually experienced them. I transported myself to their experiences and let the words crawl out of my throat and claw through my hands onto paper. The work you are about to read is my invocation of these experiences and these voices, some dead and some alive, that have endured untold pain and trauma — trauma that has impacted and changed each of them forever.

Most of the women in these stories are family members, and some of them are women I learned of through family members. Their stories have haunted me since reception. Many of their pains are rooted in larger cultural phenomena, while some are rooted in the inevitable but nevertheless unjust nature of the human experience. They speak to the great pains that, historically, women have been tasked to bear.

As I began writing these narratives, I realized that, without a sizable amount of context, much about these experiences would be lost upon many readers. Thus, I've inserted some informational chapters to contextualize the stories herein. They highlight a country of which many are unaware and illuminate the unique issues that it faces. You will find that some of these issues directly translate into larger experiences of collective trauma. I hope that this is apt bedding for you to rest upon while you live these experiences with me.

I am a first-generation American. I am mixed-race. I am a woman. I am a Muslim. These are the stories of women who make up my understanding of myself, as well as of those whose stories were never told, but that I offer to you now.

■ ■ ■

Pansy

2012

DO YOU KNOW WHAT IT FEELS LIKE TO HOLD FIRE BETWEEN your lungs? A heat that scalds you with every inhalation and screams with every breath you release. Swimming throughout your chest both playfully and menacingly. Sometimes cleansing in the way of sacred flames over which priests have sung in Sanskrit. But mostly defacing, like slurs painted on a house of worship. Your body is a hate crime.

The heat in my chest began as a small kindling. The kind of kindling we all carry with us bit by bit with every coming and going — our first failure, our first heartbreak, our first loss. I daresay I was born with bright embers inert in my body. Sparkling, golden cinders that somehow extend no light. When my mother gave me life she also gave life to this wretched fire, which is probably why she often lamented about how difficult the labor was. When she first swaddled me in her arms, she must have known that my beginnings were inauspicious.

My father, Edward Chu-A-Kong, was never married to my

mother even though she bore him three children. He had his own wife and they had their own four children. My mother, Inez Ferguson, never cared to be his wife and happily raised their three children without any kind of romantic objections. She was like that. The kind of person who could resist the inclinations that surrounded her. She owned a rum shop in our small village in Leguan, but she never had a drink in her life. She had children for a married man, but loved him silently without ever asking for more time than what he offered. When he died just two years after I was born, she was never with another man again. When I ran away to New York and left my only child with her in the village, she contentedly received her and raised her for the years that I was gone. Like someone had delivered the mail and she said, "Fine, just set it down right there." It was as though the world did not interest her because she secretly carried everything she needed within her, which would probably explain the smirk that was often found resting on her face like a comfortable houseguest. She contained all of the world's secrets. She rejected desire.

My father belonged to one of the first handful of families to migrate to the British West Indies from China. I cannot remember what he looked like, and the photos we have of him are scarce. But I am told that he had deeply hooded eyes and a Fu Manchu mustache, the kind that starts on the corners of the mouth and extends downward past a clean-shaven jaw. My construction of his face is a fusion of these vague descriptions and the paintings of men on randomly encountered Chinese ceramic ware. Although I didn't know him, I knew his mother, my grandmother, very well. My grandmother, whom we lovingly called Chapo, was a mere four and a half feet tall with black hair that cascaded gallantly to the ground when she removed the dozens of pins that kept it up in a neat bun like a glistening onyx crown. She brushed her thick tresses one hundred times each night; it was a spectacle that I watched with widened, bright eyes in complete disbelief that a woman so small could carry such a large mass atop her head, while my own hair has always been thin and unceremonious.

Chapo loved cats and kept many in her home as pets. They pranced and climbed and rolled all about her living spaces in a crescendo of playful chaos, their narrow tails almost always extended upright in the air. One night, as she was in the middle of her one hundred brushstrokes, one of her cats got tangled in the bulk of her hair and scratched her leg while trying to set itself free. Over the days that followed, the scratch bred a septic infection that flowered in first red and then green rashes, and ultimately killed her. Such a peculiar life with such a peculiar end.

My mother was Black, Scottish, and Indian. Her hair was dense with African heritage, and her eyes were hazel but later became gray like foggy European skies. For much of her life, her skin was a confused bronze, which we learned was actually ivory white after her first year living in New York and out of the Guyanese sun. She raised me and my two elder brothers with an alloy of draconian and affectionate parenting methods. We received both kisses and beatings. Both love and disdain. When Alzheimer's and Parkinson's absorbed her body, leaving her unable to speak for over ten years, I cared for her in my Queens, New York home like she was my baby. Bathing her, feeding her, loving her. She was the only parent I ever knew.

As for my father's proper wife, I've no clue what she was like. I just knew that she was an Amerindian, living in the interior with their four children. The Native peoples were strange to us, just as we village people were strange to the people in town. We called Amerindians "Buck," a phrase alluding to their perceived backwardness. They lived without schools and followed indigenous religions in which they worshiped the same trees to which we tied our hammocks. As far as my young mind could imagine, the woman married to my father lived amongst bushes and didn't own shoes. As far as I knew, she was the family my father chose, while we were the family that existed in his periphery.

When my father died of malaria, his seven children were left without him, but only one family truly felt that absence. The two families never met. Not even once. You see, some paths are just not crossed, like that of a wife and a mistress, even if it means never meeting your siblings. There is a burning in my chest that cries in agony for them. Some have strongly speculated by way of the proverbial village hearsay that his wife poisoned him when she found out about his infidelity — placed the toxins right in his food. "Dead Man Watah," as they called it. Nothing of the sort has ever been proven, and it was far too peculiar a story to ever gain any traction beyond the minds and mouths of the bored village elders — even more peculiar than my Grandma Chapo's death. After he passed, I'm not sure if I ever saw my mother grieve, though I am certain she did. Her complacency did not mean she was emotionless. Perhaps her grief translated in the fact that she never had another lover. It is only now, in my old age, that I can understand this romantic stagnation to be a form of devastation.

I experienced no such stagnation. I was engaged twice, married twice — three different lovers. I also briefly lived with an East Indian man when I migrated to New York, but that quickly ended when I found out about his wife and children in India. I refused to once again belong to a man's peripheral affections. I kicked him out with an outpour of expletives, only to see him again at my mother's funeral nearly twenty years later. I still hadn't forgiven him for reminding me of who my father was.

When I was sixteen, the burning in my chest burst in explosion. I had left my simple village life in Leguan for the first time so that I could study for the National Teacher's Exam in town. My country was in turmoil. The flames I felt scorching my consciousness matched the flames that blistered the homes and government buildings throughout the country. Supporters of the People's Progressive Party, predominantly Indian in demographic, were being massacred. Murdered in open daylight, riot after riot. I collapsed along with my country. It was my first nervous breakdown. The stress of studying and the anguish of watching innocent people die in cold murder all around me was too much. It was my first time away from village life, and I was so overcome that I had to be hospitalized. Brought back to life in a government medical facility. I can still smell the sponge bed that rested pungently beneath me, rancid in the stink of the sick who slept there before I did.

Once I reanimated myself, I propelled right back into the belly of my studies. I scored the highest in the country on the teaching exam and became the youngest person in Guyana to receive a teaching certificate with such high scores. I became a teacher in Linden and the Assistant Headmistress at Wismar Secondary School. Most importantly, I became known in Leguan as the respected Teacher Pansy.

"Teacher Pansy, how yuh do?"

"Good day, Teacher Pansy!"

"Say hello to your mommy for me, Teacher Pansy."

But in every greeting and every recognition, the images of the massacres and the smell of burning flesh stained my happiness. My pride and achievement poisoned by the memories of hate that filled the land.

I got engaged for the first time at twenty-one, just a few years after I settled into the role of Teacher Pansy, to a Chinese man who was a friend of my father's family, a short chubby man with sharp business acumen. The fire in my chest might not have found permanent lodgings within me had I married him. My life might have been very different. But, alas! My own scandals set us apart.

I quickly broke off my engagement when I realized I was pregnant, carrying the child of a Madrasan man twenty years my senior. His name was John Singh. John was born Ramlogan Singh and belonged to one of the most vibrant sects of Hinduism, characterized by sacrificial pujas and the periodic nudging of the dark powers that be. When he converted to Christianity, as many who wanted government jobs had to do, he became John Singh. I never met Ramlogan, but I loved John. When he learned I was pregnant, we had a small church wedding, and five months later I gave birth to my daughter Genevieve. My brothers often went away to French Guiana on business, so French names became my fixation. In addition to my Genevieve, John's two children from his prior marriage, John Jr. and Deborah, stayed with us now and then. I was a wife. A mom. A step-mom. I had a new life. Just like that. A new family. In the forefront, not in the outskirts of some man's love! I'd broken the curse of loneliness and rejection that my father had cast on my life.

■

John, this man who gave me so many new identities upon our marriage, is the reason it hurts to breathe. He is the reason why, now, in my old age and dementia, when I don't know what day it is or what my name is, I still remember that face. When he died in 2007, so many years after I ran away, my body shook and tears flowed — tears I didn't know I still had left for that wretched man. I couldn't imagine that I'd finally be living in a world where his existence could no longer harm me.

I didn't see it until it was in my face: both the smell of cheap rum that radiated off his skin and the fists that collided with my cheeks in his drunken stupors. I'd run home to my mother for safety, only to return home with him after his sober repentance. He'd cry and even sing to me on the radio, vowing to never hurt me again. But it became more frequent. More violent. More murderous. Once he picked up a hammer and aimed to bring it down on my skull. By some miracle, or just the inadequacy of his drunken faculties, my two-year-old daughter jumped and stilled his hand. On another occasion, not even my child could help me as he beat me so mercilessly on the outside stairs that my second child left my body with black blood flooding down my legs. From the windows of the neighboring homes, I could see tiny eyes peering through tiny openings in white lace drapes as my eyes rolled backward in pain.

How does one escape a tragedy so vast? In a village where this is as normal as the morning crows? Where men are expected to drink rum while the women are expected to prepare their meals, make their babies, and take their beatings? Where the police would send me right back home in a chorus of guffaws if I sought their help? Me! A Headmistress at the very school that their children attended! They would send me back home! How does one challenge this? Before I learned all about U.S. Visas from a woman in the vegetable market as we picked okra, I tried a more sinister escape in the face of dejection. The burning in my chest waltzed upon every corner of my body.

Just weeks after my miscarriage, I snuck out of bed with undetected ease, as John was too drunk to notice in his comatose slumber. I grabbed my Jenny and, with her asleep as I carried her on my hip, I walked. In the deep night in Leguan, crickets, frogs, and myriad amphibians sang choruses into the inky black sky. The rustling of leaves from the overhead palm trees punctuated their verses. It was through this village melody that I walked in sure and even steps on the sand and mud roads and stopped at the trench, filled with the same dingy and dark water that I once played in as a child. I bent my knees and propelled, Jenny jolted awake in my tight embrace, for only immersion in deep waters could quell this burning. My escape felt so sweet.

■

I wish I could say I had an epiphany that stopped me. That my own logical thinking and faculties saved my life and preserved my child. But no such thing is part of my story. I did not resist. I gave in. There wasn't a prayer or Bible verse that could heal the sickness that owned my body. It was a sickness much like possession. My body was no longer my own. It was owned by my pain. It guided my feet to the watery end it yearned for.

By some will of the universe, a villager was awake at that hour when even the mosquitoes are too tired to bite.

He was a young man who was probably partaking in the very rum that led me to seek death. When he snatched me by the wrist and I felt the bumps of his calluses on my skin, I grappled and tossed myself about, soon kicking and flailing with my long legs as I tried to break free. He was ruining my escape. "Hey! Hey! Hey!" He shouted as he struggled to keep me still. Jenny shrieked in horror as she awoke from her toddler's sleep to find herself in the middle of a physical struggle in the open night. Soon he contained us both in his sturdy arms, and I could feel the stubble that blanketed his cheeks graze my bare shoulder as he steadied me to the ground and took Jenny from my surrendered arms. In this struggle, he restored my life. My daughter and I were saved. The very first baptism sanctified by the avoidance water.

After Dawan saved me, I was hospitalized for what I would learn was my second nervous breakdown. My psyche had become so much more fragile since the last. I stopped giving in to John's tears and remorse and moved back in with my mother. John sang on the radio nearly every day for many years; the whole of Guyana probably would have paid me to forgive him if for nothing more than to end the misery he imposed upon everyone else via airwaves. I never heard his sorry songs. Instead, I avoided the radio altogether. Even after I left Leguan and moved to New York, his implorations and public grief continued. Singing and begging and groveling for his wife and daughter to return home. When Jenny got married years later in New York, her in-laws smiled when they realized who I was. "Oh my! You are the one that man sang to every day on the radio!"

In my second attempt at escaping the seemingly

inescapable, I left Jenny with my mother in the wretched village and fled to make a life of my own. If I could survive earning my credentials in a politically ravaged Guyana, I was sure I could start all over again and be fine. I had to leave Teacher Pansy behind. This country could not save me. It did not value or respect me. It only fed the fire that tried to kill me. This country tried to convince me that I was alright, as I stood in front of it alight in flames.

■

In New York I found work in the fashion industry; or at least that's how I packaged it in order to mask the fact that I calculated figures all day — technically for a women's clothing company! I purchased a home in Queens and sent for my daughter some years later when she was twelve. She and my mother moved in with me; just us three women in our own home, creating our own safety. I had fleeting lovers, I had income, and I had a home. I had freedom. I was no longer the weak Teacher Pansy. I was a force to be reckoned with, with my city job by day and my famed baking business by night. In the daylight I took the train to arrive at a fancy Manhattan office where I had a cubicle and a desk and a computer. In the quiet of the night, I baked traditional wedding cakes for Guyanese couples living in the neighborhood. Towering black cakes with regal icing and decorative toppers. At the height of my popularity, I had orders from as far south as Florida and as far north as Canada. I was a businesswoman who laughed and cussed and earned. Nothing could stop me in this new life. I could forget everything, including that night with my daughter when I tried to drown us both.

But the burning in my chest always preserves the memories

of the things that nearly ended me. Sometimes when it is very quiet in the still of the night, I can hear the frogs and the crickets and the rustling of palm leaves, even during dead New York winters. The bed will feel like it has been pulled from underneath me with my stomach forming knots in the way that it does when one is free falling. The smell of a rancid hospital sponge bed will fill my nostrils.

And then I wake up. Reminded that he is dead, along with my father and my mother and that history.

The burning in my chest hums wickedly with delight as I catch my breath.

Domestic Violence in Guyana

In Guyana, domestic violence transcends racial and socioeconomic lines. It creeps into homes throughout the country, throughout history, cruelly deconstructing the most intimate facets of human life. While there are laws on the books prohibiting and criminalizing domestic violence, these laws are hardly enforced. Those most tasked with the responsibility of implementing and executing these laws, like judges and police officers, do a great disservice to Guyanese women through their complacency and seeming disinterest. Implementation especially suffers in the interior of the country where there is substantially less development and police presence.

To further compound this issue, Guyanese

courthouses are often filled with staff who are insensitive to the plights of the abused women who even make it to a judicial venue. Regressive cultural norms suggest that women who are beaten by their husbands must have done something to deserve it; beatings are a disciplinary necessity with which municipalities need not interfere. In the same vein, these cultural norms also convey that male victims of domestic violence are undeserving of help; they are laughable if they can allow a woman to abuse them.

Similarly, Guyanese police stations are often staffed by officers lacking both sensitivity and an apt understanding of the laws they are supposed to enforce, even though domestic violence training is an integral component of the police training curriculum. In cases where the police do take action against domestic violence offenses, a small bribe payment can easily make those offenses dissipate into nonexistence. According to the most recent retrievable statistics, in 2015, the Guyana Police Force received 2,170 reports of domestic violence throughout the country, yet from these cases, only 1,131 people were charged.[1]

The result of this impunity is an environment in which victims of domestic violence have virtually no outlets for relief outside of those that they forge for themselves. These can include escaping their homes with the help of loved ones, fleeing Guyana for a country that is less hospitable to violence of this nature, or even suicide.

Today, there are a handful of NGOs working to both assist victims of domestic violence and directly impact the way existing domestic violence laws are implemented throughout the country. One NGO, Help and Shelter (www.hands.org.gy) has made especially large strides in the pursuit of affecting change in the terrain of domestic violence. Help and Shelter's mission is to transform prevailing attitudes toward domestic violence in Guyana. In fulfilling this goal, the NGO has worked to provide conflict resolution outlets for families and escape options for victims trying to leave their abusive households. They also regularly carry out educational campaigns and provide counseling and shelter for abused women for up to six months. The organization was formally launched throughout the Caribbean on November 26, 1995, which was the United Nations' International Day for the Elimination of Violence Against Women.

A current initiative being undertaken in pursuit of the eradication of domestic violence in Guyana by the NGO Caribbean Development Foundation is the implementation of the Cascadia Protocol. This protocol makes the following recommendations to the Guyanese government in terms of transforming the way that domestic violence is reported and the way that domestic violence victims are regarded by the institutions meant to protect them:

"1. Domestic violence units to be implemented at every police station in Guyana.
2. Police service to provide security for shelters, i.e., camera monitoring and periodic drive-by checks.
3. Mandatory reporting of suspected cases of domestic violence by medical and health professionals.

4. Implementation of a data collection system on domestic violence in the health sector, police service, and judiciary.

5. Mandatory counseling for perpetrators of domestic violence.

6. Implementation of age appropriate domestic violence awareness programs in secondary schools.

7. Establishment of a capital fund by the government of Guyana for the maintenance of shelters.

8. Implementation of the one percent transfer of income tax system, to be transferred to public organizations working to eradicate violence against women.

9. Provision of transitional housing by the government of Guyana to shelters working with victims of domestic violence.

10. Creation of a Caribbean Regional Witness Protection Program for victims of domestic violence assessed as being at risk of being murdered by their spouse / partner."[2]

Despite the existing advocacy efforts being pursued in the fight to combat domestic violence, a recent survey conducted by The Americas Barometer shows that the Guyanese population has a relatively high level of acceptance of abuse, especially when compared to other countries in the Americas.[3] Interviews for the survey were conducted between the years 2006 and 2014; one finding was that 35.6% of those interviewed would approve or understand if a man hit his wife because she had been unfaithful. In order to target this cultural concern at its root, Help & Shelter plans to conduct workshops in schools in order to teach children about the harms of domestic violence and to create safe spaces for them to discuss the experiences that they may already have with respect to violence in their homes.

Outside of the spectrum of grassroots efforts and domestic law, Guyana also has obligations as a member of the international legal community through its commitment to the Convention on the Elimination of All Forms of Discrimination Against Women (CEDAW). Most concisely, CEDAW defines what constitutes discrimination against women and outlines an agenda for national action to end that discrimination. This convention thus establishes a framework through which domestic violence must be addressed and commits signatory nations to undertaking initiatives conducive to those goals.[4]

Notwithstanding the promise of flowery international obligations, domestic violence reform in Guyana fails to garner the commitment that is necessary for true improvements to be made as it continues to be designated as a private, personal matter with which the state should not meddle. Most simply, this is because Guyana is plagued by what are considered greater evils than domestic violence, including gang-related violence and a thriving international drug-trafficking industry. Indeed, both of these threats serve as the causes of high murder rates, especially the persistence of a robust and seemingly impenetrable drug trade. In aggregate, these national issues are simply far too great for a developing country like Guyana to carry on its back all at once. While the country remains selective concerning the dragons that it is able to slay, thus leaving domestic violence on the back burner of its national development, families throughout the country are left to suffer as they wait for their government to realize their pertinence or as they wait for independent efforts, like NGOs, to emerge from the shadows. After decades of legislative efforts and international commitments, victims of domestic violence still have to forge their own outlets for relief, all while their government is sufficiently armed with the tools needed to protect them but lacking the morale to use those tools to properly protect the abused.

■ ■ ■

Inez

1947

A GLASS OF EL DORADO RUM IS JUST UNDER THE COST OF a new dress and matching rubber slippers. Most patrons opt for the cheaper whiskeys: a few dollars a glass, even less for a swig. The ones with very little money buy a single swig of high wine at my shop and then run to the chemist's shop to buy an even cheaper jug of rubbing alcohol or methylated spirits to drink at home and finish the job. Many of them later die from eroding innards.

Rum is a steady venture for village men who seek to forget. It kept my countryside shop afloat. As soon as the sun began to walk to bed, government and field workers alike would flock to my counter. The men respected me deeply. After all, I was the dispenser of their escapes. The women celebrated me because I knew exactly how much each of their men could consume before becoming intolerable.

I'd send Vish home after three glasses of scotch and Ronald after just one shot of high wine. Ramsingh could manage as much as an entire bottle of the golden rum before he started cussing my pet cat, and if Sheldon had anything in excess of two glasses of Pusser's, he would surely stumble home to beat Vashtie while the children cried in the kitchen. I maintained this delicate chemical order; I was revered as the balancer of scales.

I ran the best rum shop in Leguan and yet never tasted a drop of it. The shop comprised the lower level of my home while I lived with my family on the second floor. My father's obsession with the rum and its history tipped me off on the master idea. I'd seen how much men would pay, how much they would give up, just for a glass. I'd learned how the Europeans made this country into their own prized cash cow on my grandparents' backs, distilling what was called one of the finest golden rums they'd ever seen: liquid gold, they called it. Yes, we found gold on our plantations and then it was snatched from our hands and called a "discovery."

My grandmother was a Negro slave on a sugar plantation and bore a child for her Scottish overseer. Ignorant of the treasure that was just beneath her rough and tired feet, she gave birth on the very earth that remained pregnant with wealth, the treasure that would bolster years of riches and industry for this colony. She gave her new daughter the surname of her Scottish master, and thus Virginia Ferguson, my mother, became known as the woman with white skin and deep brown hair that fanned like tropical trees. I inherited her hair, her skin, and striking eyes.

When the Negroes finally became free, the Indians were dumped on the Guyanese coast with their bare feet and covered heads. They were the new wave of labor for the sprawling empire of sugar and rum that was sprouting from the ground like curious worms. Their women were the next to be pillaged, a new generation soon to be born with mysterious eyes and strange complexions. My mother married an Indian, Seegobin Rupnauth, and when she died in my childhood, he cared for me without the help of any other woman. I have always said I would be like him. That if God ever took my lover away, I would never seek another. How strange he must have looked, carrying me on his hip, this not-white-not-black-not-Indian child with no features matching his except the round bulb of my nose.

I left school after my third year of primary school. But Daddy was sure to take me to church each Sunday. The pews were always filled with new converts, Daddy included, who needed to accept the new God in order to secure government jobs. Their baptisms meant leaving the fields. The faithful Hindus remained on those fields, and they would come into great wealth once the British finally left the country. A reward for staying devoted to their ancient deities.

But Daddy loved the church beyond it being a ticket out of farm work. He loved congregating with others. Praying, chatting, and singing. Some of my favorite hymns were also Daddy's favorites.

> What a friend we have in Jesus,
> All our sins and griefs to bear!
> What a privilege to carry
> Everything to God in prayer!
> Oh, what peace we often forfeit,
> Oh, what needless pain we bear,
> All because we do not carry
> Everything to God in prayer!
>
> —Joseph M. Scriven, 1855

When Daddy became sick in his elderly age, I sang this in his room as I tidied the space. I cared for him meticulously, just as

I cared for my own kids and just as he had cared for me. I fed him, washed him, and sang to him until he died, exactly the way my daughter Pansy would care for me during my last days in America. Giving up her demanding job for a flexible one, all to be home and care for me when the health aides ended their shifts. Covering my face in kisses before bed each night.

Daddy was the one who told me about the liquid gold and how the Englishmen introduced the colony to the use of distilleries. About how the Royal Navy consumed it with abandon as the colony grew richer and richer. And just like that, at the turn of my adulthood, I opened up shop armed with nothing more than Daddy's stories and my few years of schooling. I could read and add. I was sufficient.

I sold rum as yellow as my famed gold tooth and never drank a drop of that blood-stained treasure. It was my Koh-i-noor diamond, though I barely lived above poverty, until it became the cancer of my daughter's marriage years later. An angel and a beast in one serving.

In between serving drinks, I'd settle quarrels, advise women on their marriage prospects, and direct the young people on how to frame their futures. Me, with no education and just a simple shop in my possession. Yet nearly every second hour there was something to tend to. *Ineez!* They would cry, always pronouncing my name with a long "e" sound. The Indians called me Ineez Rupnauth, while the Africans and the few remaining European descendants called me Inez Ferguson. The former acknowledged the man who raised me, the latter forcefully reminded me of the darkness of how I came to be.

"Ineez, I need your help!"

"Ineez, should I sell the house?"

"Ineez, I cannot live another day with this man!"

The questions and heartaches and fears all wound up at my unqualified doorstep, throbbing before my tired feet. But just as I'd done for my children, I hoisted each problem up and nursed them, rendering advice like a dignified village sage.

"Buy di grains at Bourda, it's thirty percent cheaper there."

"Sell di house, but not to him. He'll never give you what it's worth."

"Oh, darling, he only said that you chew like wan mountain goat. He still finds you quite beautiful!"

It was a matter of irony that my livelihood would rely on a substance that I only understood in theory. Quite the same kind of irony that, while I was a dealer of this abstract gold, the father of my three children mined sincere gold and diamonds. And, boy, did he have sincere money to prove it. He was a pork knocker; that's what they called the Chinese miners along the Mazaruni River. They ventured into the interior, hauling all of their food behind them, mainly salted pork. The pork attracted so many flies that the miners were constantly slapping them to rid their provisions of pests. And so the spectators called them pork knockers, a term that has endured for decades.

The pork knockers were a thing of folklore in our history. It was a quandary how they were able to withstand the conditions of living in Guyana's jungles, with its bizarre vegetation and mysterious wildlife yet to be fully discovered. Somehow, Edward Chu-A-Kong, a handsome descendant of Chinese migrants, not only thrived in the jungles, but seamlessly weaved in and out of the village and the jungle — each time giving me a new child. Edward had a mustache that extended past his chin on either side, accented by small sprouts of chin hair. His face narrow and his eyes deeply hooded. When my daughter was of school age, she began to imagine that the drawings on the Chinese porcelain we saw in the town markets were portraits of her father's family. She held the plates and ran her small fingers over the painted grooves while I hurriedly collected flour and cassavas and grains.

After three long visits from Edward we had three children: Colin, Boston, and Pansy. His face danced blatantly upon theirs as though he made them on his own. Colin, my eldest, had a narrow face and wide shoulders. In his adulthood he would comb his hair back in a sleek hump on his head, a style that the women in France adored when he traveled there on business. Boston, my second son, had a face that made you remember the innocent joys of childhood. His face round and always smiling like the famed laughing Buddha with the round belly that devotees rubbed for good luck. Pansy had a slender face like her brother Colin and grew to be very tall and with catlike features, including a modest button nose and small hooded eyes. My three Chinese children with no Chinese father to make sense of how they came out looking the way they did.

When Edward left, I knew this meant he was going home to his wife, a native woman living in the interior of the country. He wasn't just going back to his mining. This was more than business. They had their own children and their own separate life in that realm of nature that people regarded as backward and treacherous. Unlike Edward, she never left the jungle. I never even learned her name. I just knew that she was the native woman that he took when he first came to mine gold. And that is how she came to be known by the village people. The Buck Lady. Over the years, dozens of Amerindians would slowly leave the interior to join us along the coast. Over the years, more and more of them would even venture beyond these nearby villages and into the towns and cities. There would be many, many more Buck Ladies in our village in later years. But Edward's mysterious wife, the one we never got to see, she was our very first Buck Lady.

He never ended his marriage with her, and we never married. Edward was married to his work. He was not committed to either home but, rather, to his accumulation of diamonds and golden bars. I remained in my sphere while his wife remained in hers, both of us only imagining what the other was like. Daddy told me that the Amerindians were wild and only wore enough cloth to cover their lower organs. He laughed and said they didn't own shoes and that they danced to ward off evil spirits.

"He wife must have she children sleep pon tree branch," Daddy once cried before spiraling into a laughing fit that reminded me of a chicken gasping for air before I snapped its neck for curry.

"Ineeeez, you hear wha meh say? Tree branch!"

I mustered up a giggle and replied, "Don't mind how bird vex, he can't vex with tree!"

It was a proverb we often recounted about unchangeable circumstances. Daddy was upset for me, but, thankfully, not with me. He didn't know or understand why Edward didn't marry me, or why I had three of his children without protest. He didn't understand why Edward never shared any of his extensive and wealthy mining empire with me and the children. And so he condemned the native family that did receive the boons of his legacy. He damned them all in the package of good humor. "Don't mind how bird vex, dad. The bird can't be angry about something he cannot change."

When Edward died, the entire village blamed the Buck Lady, even though it was pretty well settled that he succumbed to malaria and corresponding complications in the jungle.

"She nah must poison he?"

"Them nah like country people like we!"

"Yuh see how dem Buck people stay?"

"Di Buck Lady feed he Dead Man Watah!"

When he died, his wife refused to carve us even a sliver of his riches. She knew that her children's half siblings lived in poverty and that my youngest, Pansy, was but weeks old. But she couldn't bear to acknowledge that we existed, that we, too, had a right to him.

The Chu-A-Kong family had a thriving fishing business on the coast and a booming jewelry business in Georgetown. They were one of the first Chinese families to migrate to the British West Indies and they made their migration to this colony worthwhile. Whatever legacy they had in China, they tripled in this land of gold. When Edward's wife decided that I couldn't benefit from any part of it, I didn't challenge her. Not for a single second. Not for a single penny or diamond or golden nugget or can of fish. Daddy continued to curse unmoving trees.

■

"I spoke to her. His wife," Tai Ling told me in an almost whisper one afternoon. I knew it couldn't be good news when her voice became low and afraid.

Her feet were slightly swaying. They didn't touch the floor when she sat up in the splintering wooden chair by the front window of my home. She looked so much like Edward. They both had crow's feet that fanned like whiskers despite being too young for them. Their skin like boiled milk, fair with a translucent layer of discoloration on top from the years in the Guyanese heat.

Tai Ling was Edward's aunt. My boys lovingly called her

Aunty Sill. The Chinese were no exception to the colony's tradition of right names and home names. Official identities and personal ones. She lived a far way from our rural Leguan home with her sister in Annandale, a town heavily populated with Chinese migrants and their descendants. When she visited us, she had to travel by boat—one of the three that were scheduled daily to dock in Leguan. On this day, she came by way of the very last boat for the night and would not be able to return home until morning. I didn't realize this was calculated, that what she had to say would require more than a short exchange over salted biscuits and tea in flinted tin cups.

She came to make arrangements.

"Will she come? So we can talk?" I asked as I stacked and restacked the same four plates in the cupboard.

"No," Tai Ling replied curtly. "She is being unreasonable! She won't speak to anyone. If she has opened her mouth it is only to say that she will never speak to you. I can show you the letter she sent me!"

"Will she send anything?" I asked dismissively as I continued washing the same plate for the third time, the yellow cleaning rag worn and ripping in the center.

"She said to tell you that you will never have a right," Tai Ling said with downturned eyes.

"That is fine," I whispered as my eyes narrowed. I put down the plate, by now scratched from my tempered scrubbing, and dried my hands on my favorite purple baroque printed skirt with the fraying hemline. In short steps, I trudged toward Tai Ling, my children's favorite Great Aunt, and finally sat down in the creaking chair across from her.

"We will manage, Sill," I told her assuredly. I grasped her frail, bony hand with aging brown spots in my own. My fingers pruned from the plate that would never get clean.

"How, with three children?" she said in a small voice that felt like velvet. She gazed at me with her head slightly tilted.

"I will just have to work harder in the shop."

"Your father is sick!" she exclaimed.

"And I will take care of him too!" I boomed in retort. Tears began to swell over my eyes. I went back to the dishes. Didn't she know I was the balancer of scales?

"Let me help you."

"I don't want any of your money."

"Don't be silly, Ineez!"

"I am fine without his money! You do not need to go against your family for me!"

"Fine," she said in defeat of the truth that I had just spit up. "It won't be money then."

"Then what?"

"We never see these children, you know," her voice trailing away like a candle just put out.

"My poor nephew is gone and we don't get to see any of his children. We cannot just go into the jungle to see the others! It's dangerous! And just a few hours here in the countryside is never enough."

"But we cannot afford to come to town to see you so often. And I have the shop to tend to every day. I cannot leave here. It is my home."

"I know that. And that's why I came to ask you..." she began cautiously.

She rose out of her seat and walked toward me at the sink. Her long, black *changpao* grazed the flaking wood floor. I felt her small hand on my right arm as I gazed out of the window while gripping the sides of the sink. My shoulders protruded upward as I remained in a stance of concentration.

"Give me Boston," she finally said.

I turned my head swiftly, glaring at her in disbelief. Surely she didn't ask me to give her my son. My son with the face of the Buddha.

"What?"

"Please. Let me take Boston. You keep your eldest child and your youngest. Colin and Pansy will stay with you. But please, please, give us Boston. Let us raise him."

We stood in silence for what seemed like hours but was only a matter of seconds. Her peculiar arrival made sense now. Her large canvas bag, which poorly hid her overnight dressings, sat guiltily next to the doorframe. The air suddenly felt unreasonably thick. I could not breathe. My chest began to rise and fall, first slowly, then quickly in frenzy. Suddenly she placed her arms over my shaking shoulders.

"Let us take care of him. It will lighten your load. We have to care for these children together!"

"I cannot just send my child to live in town! He only knows this village."

"Oh, Ineez, he is young and will learn the town quickly! And he will be cared for and you will be able to care for Colin and Pansy better. Isn't that what matters?"

It was unfair. The woman in the jungle got to keep her babies. Was I too illegitimate to be deserving of my family? How could I fail so miserably at balancing my own scales?

"We'll come home often! We aren't hiding him away forever, silly girl. Come now. Just send him to live with his aunties and his Grandma Chapo," on and on she continued to reassure me that this was normal and good and fine. But this was not normal. The balancer of scales knew this would not be fine.

"And his school fees?" I quizzed.

"We will take care of it from what we have. Please, Ineez . . . it is best for all of them."

My youngest child, Pansy, was just a baby. I could barely find time to nurse her. My breasts often screamed as I worked the shop, producing milk that I had no time to serve. It was unfair that I couldn't keep all of my children. But it was also unfair to deny them a solution. Placing your child's life before your own. Their happiness before your own well being. It is a difficulty that all mothers have to accommodate. Even the balancer of scales.

And so we packed his things in the morning. It was too much to sort through with just moonlight and candlelight so we scurried to bed, me anxious about sending my son on the boat heading to town and Tai Ling impatient for the sunrise that would grant her custody of my little laughing Buddha.

He was elated when we told him the next morning. He counted down the seconds before he would be on the boat and in his new town. What does a child of five years know beyond the fact that he is going to town? Does he know just what it means for one to leave their mommy? I put his very best clothes in his school bag, a red sack adorned with yellow star appliqués. Tai Ling said she would buy him the rest of whatever he needed when they reached Annandale. She assured me of it. She would mind him.

I walked with them to the dock. Boston's small legs fluttered in hurried steps. I held Pansy on one shoulder as she slept, and dug the skin next to my thumb with my free right hand. We stood waiting for the boat to traipse into the dock, overflowing with angry patrons cursing about the delays and bumpy waters.

My shop was busy that night with all those men eager to purge the stress and tension of their voyage. I poured copious glasses of liquid gold. It was the drink of the hour. The imported stuff didn't stand a chance. Glasses filled with hurt and joy, depending on the eyes from which you looked at them. A swig here. Three glasses there. One patron, clearly in the political arena, as told by his red tie and the government pin attached to his jacket lapel, even ordered an entire bottle. "A bottle of rum, Miss Ineez. And two empty glasses."

By the end of the night, my chest was aching and brimming with milk while Pansy cried in hunger, dampening my clothes like a bottle that hadn't been corked properly. As I packed away the bottles into the locked cabinets, I thought of my grandmother. A slave birthing her child on a secretly treasured land, unaware of what was owed to her. The liquid gold swayed sensuously in the last bottle as I packed it away, the glass clanging with the bottles beside it. I slammed the cabinet so hard that the room shook. My son Colin came running down the dusty, creaking wooden stairs, sure that I had fallen down. Pansy's wails awoke the entire street.

A Brief History of African Slavery in Guyana

Guyana's enslaved Africans were first brought to the small country by the Dutch and later by way of the British West India Company. The slave ships arrived in ports in Berbice, Essequibo, and the Demerara, and auctions were held during which plantation owners inspected naked Africans to discern if they were healthy enough to work on their grounds. Families were commonly separated during this dehumanizing auction process, as slave owners cared very little for the family cohesion of their purchases.[5] To further divide the African slaves, members of the same tribe were strategically separated in the auctioning process so as to ensure that they would not come together to rebel. They were purchased along with groups that spoke different dialects. They were purchased in a state of division.

The African slaves, many of them Muslim and others from various tribal spiritual traditions, were prevented from practicing their own religions or communing in worship in general. Later, however, Christian missionaries were allowed on plantations, and Christianity became the prevalent religion among the Afro-Guyanese.

A system of Colorism also plagued the African slaves within the structure of their plantation life. Along a spectrum of complexions, lighter skinned Africans and mulattoes were treated more favorably by their European overseers than their darker counterparts. This created deep division between the slaves on the plantations and pitted them against each other as each struggled for their own power and survival.

Through a series of uprisings, the slaves revolted against their oppressors in hopes of securing their freedom. The Berbice Uprising of 1763 is noted as one of the greatest events in Guyana's anti-slavery movement. During this uprising, nearly 3,000 African men, led by a slave named Cuffy, revolted against their European owners by setting plantations on fire and recruiting other slaves to join their efforts. With assistance from neighboring French and British colonial powers, the slave uprising was defeated in 1764. A statue of Cuffy currently sits in Georgetown, Guyana, in the Square of the Revolution. The anniversary of the Berbice Uprising, February 23, has been commemorated since 1970 as Guyana's Republic Day.

The second major uprising was the Demerara Revolution of 1823. This uprising involved nearly 10,000 African slaves, headed by a father and son who decided to revolt against their masters on what was known as the Success Plantation. During this uprising, many plantation owners were killed, and the British were strongly impacted by the financial losses incurred.

Slavery was officially abolished in Guyana in 1834, and after the Africans left the plantations and formed their own homes, the lost slave labor was eventually replaced by indentured laborers from India.

■ ■ ■

Bibi Shareefa

1966

WHEN I WAS BORN THE WORLD WAS ON FIRE. BLOOD oozed into every crevice of the earth, and you could see the stains of suffering wherever you turned. I was a wartime baby, which I suppose is why I've always been so petite. Tiny, in fact. When I was nine months pregnant with my first child I was only ninety pounds and just under five feet tall. My cousin Zoreen is small just like me; when she was pregnant she fell every time the baby kicked! It was the British ships that brought the staple foods of my upbringing to the Guyanese coast, and when those ships were attacked we got nothing to replace the rations that were either scorched by enemy fire or sank to the bottom of the Atlantic. While many attach the melodies of nursery rhymes to the memories of their childhood, my generation largely leaned upon the melodies of the war songs we learned in school: folk songs from England and Ireland.

Oh, Danny boy, the pipes, the pipes are calling
From glen to glen, and down the mountain side.

The summer's gone, and all the roses falling,
It's you, it's you must go and I must bide.
But come ye back when summer's in the meadow,
Or when the valley's hushed and white with snow,
I'll be here in sunshine or in shadow, —
Danny boy, I love you so!

—Frederic Weatherly, 1910

When the Second World War ended, I thought our food would be more steady. But in my adulthood, President Burnham banned many of the staples of the Indian diet. There was no flour for roti, no potato for our curries. In harder times, we barely had dried peas to boil down for dhal. Our stomachs mourned for heritage. I was destined to remain small.

I am one of fourteen children. My mother gave birth to her last child just months before I gave birth to my first. The older ones raised the younger ones while my parents oversaw the operations like pleased regional managers. It sounds like chaos, and it certainly was. But we loved each other dearly despite the inevitable organized mayhem that ensued daily in our home.

I guess it wouldn't come as much of a surprise for me to say that it was both the happiest and saddest day of my life to leave this home as a bride. I was just eighteen years old, and my small frame could barely hold up my huge gown. My husband, just a few months older than I, would thereafter go on to always call me Little Woman.

"Where is that Little Woman?" Basheer would ask jokingly when he would return home from work in the evenings. "Where is she?"

Marriage was something I didn't even realize I wanted. In fact, I was decidedly not interested in getting married when the offer presented itself. I was consumed with becoming a talented seamstress. I was the best in my class at knitting and stitching and regularly knit myself beautiful sweaters, dresses, and scarves. Once, I saved my money and bought an exquisite material that I learned from the elderly shopkeeper was called fale. It was elegant and shiny, and after weeks of stitching by hand, I was able to make a charming dress out of it that I kept for years.

One evening, while attending a function with my family, Basheer's parents caught sight of me. Such was the way of marriage back then. The parents must fall in love before you have a chance to. The next day, they immediately came home to speak to Daddy.

"We want Anita," they said. Anita is my home name. The very use of it on their tongues was a deliberate expression of their desire to make me part of their own home. "Please send a picture of her to show our son."

Daddy knew I didn't have any individual pictures. Can you imagine having individual photos printed for so many children? No. We only had studio family portraits that looked more like an expansive class graduation picture with my parents always positioned prominently in the center like proud headmasters.

The very next day after their visit, Daddy took me to a photo studio alone. I hadn't a clue what was happening but happily welcomed the opportunity to have a day out of the house. I sat in the subject's chair, potent with the smell of aging leather, and the photographer grabbed my chin with his clammy fingers to position my face to the right. It seemed strange that I wouldn't be looking at the lens, but Daddy was pleased with the way the frame looked so I didn't question it. I wore the fale dress I had spent weeks stitching, believing it was fit for the occasion of having Daddy take me out all by myself. After the photo was snapped, we went to see a cowboy film while the film developed.

The cinema contained a sizable auditorium where many young boys would stay all day after buying tickets for just one show. The speakers were positioned on either end of the drop-down screen and boomed in authority once the reels began playing. Daddy mainly came to the cinema to watch his cowboy films, not like the rest of the elders who came to watch Hindi films and dance in the aisles. He loved watching the western heroes on the screen and his eyes often gleamed as he observed them with their leather boots and large hats as they galloped heroically into the sunset. When the film ended that afternoon he smiled widely with his thin lips and told me it was about time to go back to retrieve my photo. We pushed through the slow crowd exiting the cinema and took the main road back in hurried steps so as to make it back before the stores closed and the country went to sleep.

When we finally made it back to the shop, the photographer had begun packing up for the day. His door was locked, and he had chased away some folks who were knocking on the door just before we arrived, shaking his head and mouthing the words: "No. We are closed." But when we stood in front of the door, he smiled sheepishly and came to unlock it. "Come in," he said as we followed him to his counter. He was sure to lock the door again after letting us in. He retrieved a flat brown envelope from his desk and, with his skeletal fingers, peeled open the envelope and plucked a square photograph that left me in shock. It was beautiful! I could not believe it was me! Daddy was very pleased as well and immediately sent a copy to the Mohamad family to present to their son. My husband died with that picture in his wallet.

■

We married on Valentine's Day in 1960. My sister had an interested suitor as well, so we had a grand double wedding at our home. As per tradition, Daddy killed a bull to cook for our wedding guests. My husband's *bharaat* came with fourteen cars down our narrow street. Just thinking of that day still brings a happy shimmer to my eyes, like when sunlight reflects on a mirror, quickly followed by tears that sting. After the *nikkah*, our guests ate and went home. And I went to my new home with a man I didn't know and who had only seen me once aside from my studio portrait.

In the beginning of our marriage, we were merely cordial. We smiled politely at one another and shyly blushed over dinner conversations. I was thrust into the pandemonium of taking on new responsibilities in the home of my in-laws, and he was adjusting to having a new woman in his lifelong home. This was the usual course of things in an arranged marriage, something for which you can never prepare no matter how many times you are informed or advised or witness it yourself.

I had five children for Basheer Mohamad: three mischievous boys and two lovely girls. He was always jovial and upbeat, a loving husband and playful father. He loved to sing and loved his religion. Whenever he came home late at night and I would quarrel with him about the time, he would simply ignore me and sing. He would even dance if I continued to complain, just to mock my agitation. I cannot remember a single time that he was ever angry. Just always singing. He kept song lyrics in his pocket at all times, changing them only after committing the lyrics to memory. The words were scribbled on folded, lined paper in the smooth ink from his novelty pens.

He would often sing his favorite Hindi film songs in the

evenings as he walked through the wooden doorframe, or in the mornings as he got dressed, with my eldest child, Wazir, mimicking the tunes. His small mouth harmonized lyrics in a language he did not understand, a language our people had let go of long ago:

Koi jab raa na paaye, mere sang aaye
Ke pag pag deep jalaaye
Meri dosti mera pyaar.

When one does not find the path, he should come with me
And lights the path
My friendship and my love.

—"Meri Dosti Mera Pyaar," from the film *Dosti*, 1964

It is a painful injustice to translate Hindi to English. The meaning gets lost in a language so bare and unforgiving, stiff like the ships that used to bring our rations. Yet just like we needed the ships, we clutched these translations closer and closer while our grasp of the old languages of Hindi and Urdu withered away. None of this mattered, of course, to my then four-year-old, who merely sang to imitate the melodies of his father.

Basheer's favorite songs were Hindi devotional songs about mothers. He would memorize endless verses about a mother's love and selflessness, harmonizing them as though feeling every note. He adored his mother. And I cannot say that it was an unreasonable adoration. When we got married my mother-in-law was just thirty-nine years old. She was married at fourteen and started having her children at fifteen. She was a thing of beauty and light, quite fitting for her namesake, Jannah. She loved to dress up, curling her hair meticulously and applying makeup to highlight all the right angles of her beautiful, symmetrical face. I fell in love with her before I fell in love with my husband. This was the woman my husband sang about: the embodiment of a mother's love. When I finally had his children a new joy entered my heart, for I felt that when he sang his devotionals, he was maybe also singing to me: the mother of his five babies.

Then one day, just like that, everything was silenced. With an infant crying in my arms, all of the melodies were replaced with wails of devastation. The world was not quite that tender to me, to allow me to grieve with everyone else. Just as I was plunged into the world of married life, I was as swiftly catapulted into a life of tragedy. I spent all day and all night sewing clothing for income, dresses and suits for which people didn't even want to pay half a dollar despite the perfect seams, hems, and necklines. I only took brief breaks to prepare meals for the kids, often lying that I had already eaten so the portions would be sufficient. With the help of grandparents, aunts, and uncles, my children always had food and love. They knew their father through their relatives. All while I silently mourned as I sat behind my Singer sewing machine without a moment to spare worrying about whether we'd all come out of this alive. I could not spare a moment to grieve that the singing had stopped, that my life had become void of the music to which I had so sweetly become accustomed, or that my world had become so sad, so silent.

The day I became a widow I was unable to hear. People were shouting, and my children, still babies, screamed in confusion. But I could only hear his voice. Singing. When Wazir got his first guitar as a teenager, I left my sewing desk, stormed into his room and grabbed it while he was singing and strumming. I told him I couldn't take the noise. "I am trying to work!" But he just continued to strum it haphazardly and relentlessly. Didn't they know that I wasn't ready for music just yet? He continued to play and sing the same way his father did when he would greet me at the door.

■

I spent many years in deep contemplation of what exactly happened to me. In the old country where my family came from, the fate of many widowed women would be one of death. Tragically, in the very moment that their children lost their fathers, they lost their mothers as well. First, the grieving women would be robbed of colors. They would wear white every day of their life: a physical marker for the world to know that they were women whose husbands had left the world. Next, their presence would become so inauspicious that they would be isolated to the corners of their homes, lest they want to bear the shame of women fleeing their gaze for fear of attracting some of their "bad luck," or of women rushing to bathe if they so little as brushed shoulders with them by accident.

For the Muslim women it was a bit different, but also very trying. When our lovers left to be with the Creator, our *nikkah* was broken, simple as that. In the Prophet's time (peace be upon him), women often remarried after their husbands died. Their agency was intact. And yet I am still not sure which is worse? Being reminded each day of the love that has left you—in the clothes you wear and the life you live—or moving so rapidly that you must remind yourself that that person was once your companion? Failing to take the time to transition to a life you don't want to recognize? The memory of your marriage dwindling as soon as the Imam announces that the *nikkah* is broken.

Which one would I have preferred if I had the choice?

Leading the remainder of my life in somber remembrance of my husband as I sat idly in a *salwar kameez* the color of snow? Or quickly and abruptly moving on with my life in a way that felt unfair to his memory? What is the correct way to grieve? To live your life as a pseudo death? Or to continue to live through the stages and phases that you never thought you would have to weather alone? In the old country, some widows died as they surely breathed in white sarees, while others were rushed through the junctures of pain, through the process of detaching themselves from their husbands. The detachment is automatic. And yet all these oceans away, far away from the choice between a life of death or a life of life, I felt as though I had died anyway. A life of life and a life of death. Indeed, both were mine.

■

July 31, 1966. This was just weeks after the country had become independent and the world seemed to take on a happier hue than I had ever known in my life. And suddenly darkness found its way in again. My small world again on fire.

He came home one night, and we sat together in front of the house. By this time we had our own home, just a short way from my in-laws. He had just begun to tell me about his typically long day when a man walked over to us and interrupted our evening reunion.

"Basheer, you must come over. Mommy made you dinner to thank you for today." Basheer had helped this man find his way home that afternoon. This man was known for having one too many drinks and forgetting where he lived. Fortunately, there was always someone around to walk him home. And his poor mommy would thank them all with her food. Tonight it was Basheer.

"Don't go out now. It's getting late. You just got home!" I implored. We were no longer newlyweds, but I hated when he left me unnecessarily. The days were long enough when he was at work. That day had been particularly long, as he had picked up a driving job for a wedding in addition to his day shift.

"Go relax, *Boujie*," his friend said matter-of-factly, completely dismissing my concerns. "He'll be right back after dinner." The house was within walking distance of ours, so I didn't make more of a fuss. I readied myself for bed and tried to estimate how long it would take for him to walk, eat, and walk back.

There was a vehicle speeding through the streets that night. A man was driving his wife and daughter to a nearby shoe store, all while stink with drink. This driver changed my life. He made my world dark and my children question God. He summoned the hardest years of my life. He silenced the singing. When he collided with Basheer, he did not stop driving. He did not even pause or yield, convinced he had only hit a stray cow. He hit Basheer so hard that people would later recount seeing his body fly up into the air. He was killed instantly. The husband I had never even seen frown.

The news traveled throughout the estate, first to my father-in-law. Neighbors screamed to him: "Mohamad, yuh son get knock down and dead!" Such is the way of the Guyanese news pipeline, even today. Harsh and with complete disregard for the softening of transmission. In a country so ravaged by pain, things like pleasantries have no footing, even in times of tragedy. Even when it is your own tragedy.

■

I was ushered into the *masjid* the next day where his body was wrapped, per Islamic tradition, in three pieces of white cloth after being washed by a male relative. Men were singing verses from the Qur'an in overlapping voices. After the *jannazah* prayer, my mother took me to the front of the *masjid* where his body was laid. I barely saw his still face as the *Imam* quickly dismissed me, and I was forced to leave. "Um, yes, yes, your *nikkah* is now broken." In a simple fleeting moment I said goodbye to my love and became a widow. Our marriage officially broken.

Our union was witnessed with a grand celebration and hundreds of guests, but broken so swiftly and without care or tenderness. While men were able to see him many times over, his face framed in soft white cloth, I, the mother of his five children barely saw him long enough to clear the tears from my eyes. I cannot remember how he looked. I walked out of the *masjid* with my mother, and despite the summer heat, I wrapped my *chadr* tighter around my shoulders, struggling to keep warm. When the first wife of Prophet Muhammad (peace be upon him) died and he became a widower, it took him over a decade to remarry as he was so consumed in his grief. Little did I know that I would follow in that very tradition. Navigating and processing my grief in piecemeal fashion. I felt as dead as I would have in the old country. A life of life and a life of death were, indeed, both mine.

When my Basheer died, everyone grieved. My family. My friends. My village. We were all coming up for air. It was as though the world was crying, just as it was when I was born during the war. Grief everywhere I turned.

My husband's death initiated a new era. An era when things no longer scared me, for the worst had already happened, and I had no time for fear. An era when I no longer worried about my future, for the present was the only thing I could reasonably contain. One day at a time. One painful and laborious day at a time.

I sent my children to school. I taught them their religion. They were fed and they were clothed. As much as I wanted to emulate the devotional songs of motherhood that my husband used to sing, I soon realized that the composers of those songs could never know the lives of lone women. Those compositions could never capture our reality of being empty but still trying to pour out love. There was no room for worry, no time for my world to fall apart. I could not afford the luxury of trauma. I could not retreat to my room, crying and refusing to eat. Does God have time to grieve? To retreat? Such is the plight of a widowed mother: we must be the world, contain the world, and preserve the world. A silent divinity.

> Usko nahin dekha hamne kabhi
> Par iski zaroorat kya hogi
> Ai maa
> Ai maa
> Teri soorat se alag bhagwan ki soorat kya hogi
> Kya hogi
> Usko nahin dekha hamne kabhi
> We have not seen Him
> And it is not even necessary to see him
> O ma
> O ma
> We have seen you and
> God may not look any different from you in appearance
> We have not seen him

— "Usko Nahin Dekha Hamne Kabhi," from the film *Daadi Maa*, 1966

The Indo-Guyanese

The first Indians to be brought to the British West Indies, specifically to Guyana, arrived in 1838 just after the emancipation of the African slaves. Guyana, though a small country sitting on the northern coast of South America, is considered an imperative Caribbean nation. In fact, the CARICOM (Caribbean Community) Seat of Secretariat is in the country's capital of Georgetown. The first batches of indentured laborers that were sent to Guyana from India hailed from Calcutta and were among the poorest citizens of pre-partition Indian society. Indentured laborers were brought from both northern (Madhya Pradesh and Bihar) and southern (Tamil Nadu) territories of India through the British system of labor recruitment.[6] This "recruitment" often entailed kidnapping and forced detentions; many Indians were forced onto ships without any knowledge of where they were going.

It was a frenzied system borne from the realization that the newly emancipated African slaves needed to be replaced expediently. It was the kind of realization that has legitimized colonial aggression throughout the world and throughout history. This story is not a new one. Indian women were the most vulnerable to this type of recruitment. Even after being transported and stationed to work on Guyanese sugar plantations, their vulnerability persisted as many were forced to serve as sex slaves for their European managers. Violence became a steady motif for these indentured women.

Ever since their arrival in Guyana, racial tensions between the Indians and the Africans have been heavy and extensive. Much of this tension was created by the European overseers, who found great value in keeping the populations at odds with one another so as to prevent any solidarity that could overthrow the prevailing colonial powers. They told the Indians that the Africans were vile and carried diseases, and to stay away from them lest they become contaminated. They told the Africans the same thing about the Indians. So, the two groups stayed away from one another, each completely unaware of the powers that kept them from uniting and bred the animosity that would endure for generations, long after the plantations had closed and the last European ships left the shores of the promised country.

When Guyana was granted independence on May 26, 1966, the Indians and Africans were left to figure it out for themselves, a pursuit that they still have not quite figured out, as racial violence and political animosity continues to persevere throughout the country. Over the course of this history, the indentured Indians struggled to maintain their cultural identities. They eventually forged a new one altogether.

Today, the main cultural medium through which South Asian culture is retained in the Caribbean diaspora is through film and music. Bollywood films are lengthy musicals centered on the common themes of love, honor, and faithfulness to God. The soundtracks for these films are generally released prior to the release of the actual film. As a result, the musical value of a film serves as a heavy indicator of its box office success. After spending generations forging a new "Guyanese culture"—a multicultural fusion of heritage—in their new home, these films are one of the last remaining ties that the Indo-Guyanese have to their homeland, outside of certain religious traditions. Notably, the Bollywood film industry is largely representative of North Indian culture, and because this industry is the only major cultural commodity available to the Indo-Guyanese, recent generations of Indo-Guyanese possess an understanding of their ethnic roots that is deeply colored by North Indian traditions, despite the great number of South Indians that came to Guyana as laborers.

Today, the cultural contributions of Indians in Guyana are celebrated annually on May 5, in recognition of the first indentured laborers who arrived by ship on May 8, 1838. This celebration, known as Indian Arrival Day, attempts to transform the painful history of Indian "recruitment" from their homes in India to a festival of commendation for the rich Indian heritage that was introduced to the British West Indies. This festival features singing, dancing, and elaborate processions.

As the space between India and its Caribbean children grows wider, the Indo-Guyanese face sizable difficulties in the retention of their heritage. Still, there is a prevailing commitment to preserving these cultural ties among Guyana's Indian population, one that currently comprises nearly half of all Guyanese people.

■ ■ ■

Jannah

1966

MY NAME MEANS PARADISE. THE ULTIMATE GOAL OF THE devoted. Rivers of sweet water, expansive trees giving cooling shade. Our holy book says that, in *jannah*, there are no worries or stresses. Only delights and peace. It is a place where lovers never have to say goodbye. Quite a fitting name for a matriarch, really. My family has always leaned on me as their escape from cruelty. Their light to expel darkness.

I got married when I was a girl of just fourteen years old to a man of twenty. Village life necessitates these hurried marriages: an old world way of making me honest before I lose my pubescent innocence in some other way. My husband was a widower when his family asked for my hand; his first wife and first child both died during labor. I couldn't say yes or no. Only, "I do." Or as our Muslim ceremonies provide: *"Qubool hai. Qubool hai. Qubool hai."* "I agree. I agree. I agree." The three sacred affirmations in Hindi to secure the contract of an Islamic marriage. I didn't have any wedding photos. I'd never gone to school. I never learned to read. I could not write. But I knew how to cook and clean and maintain a home, a skill set that the women of my grandchildren's generation would think of as limited and stifled. But I was always so much more than that, more than just not having been enough.

I knew many chapters of the Qur'an by heart. I could speak the new English of my generation and still understand the Hindi of the old generation, a quality my grandchildren would find astounding as they observed me watching Hindi films and crying during the monologues, and howling with laughter at the jokes. All without subtitles.

It was understood that the girls of my generation were trained to be someone's other half from our very births. And so our elders arranged for the fulfillment of that destiny once we were ready for it. My own mother had no choice in this, even in her adulthood.

My father left us and I never asked why. I didn't need to. My mother happily raised her kids in a way that made us never want to ask or wonder where he was. After my own marriage, my aunty, my mother's sister, tragically died in childbirth. And, just like that, the elders decided that my mother was to marry her widowed brother-in-law so that his children, my cousins, could be properly cared for. The children became both my cousins and siblings. It is in this same way that my parents sent me to fulfill my destiny in marrying Gulam Mohamad. It was a matter of fact. A religious decree.

Despite him being a man and me just a girl, I am happy that in my young age, if I had to be given to anyone, I was given to him. Throughout my life I was treated, by my mother, my two sisters, and my brother, as a fragile baby. And to Gulam, I was a prized porcelain piece. I was the one that he minded and sheltered like a secret treasure. Other girls who married at my age did not have similar luck. They were forced into cold homes with dreadful and unforgiving in-laws. Their husbands were often brutal and had little love for the wives they barely knew. The young wives cooked and cleaned and broke their backs for families that treated them little better than slaves, and those same young wives would later have their revenge on their own *bahus* when they married off their sons. All while the men remained oblivious to the cycles of female suffering all around them. I was one of the lucky ones.

We had our first baby when I was fifteen. Never mind that I was a child myself, my children shaped my life and gave me purpose. I had ten children altogether. It would have been twelve had the twins not died. "It is called an ectopic pregnancy," the doctors explained. My two children were asleep in my fallopian tubes. Already twins in behavior. After them, my son Gul died after just a few days on this earth. My son Roshan after just two years. Each loss a tragedy I felt I would never survive. My babies tore wounds into my soul that could never be mended. Oh, I was so sure there was nothing worse than losing your baby. That thunderous dismay that envelopes your body when your breasts are ready to feed but the child is no longer there to receive. The milk soaks your clothes as your tears soak your cheeks, your body grieving to feed a child who no longer exists. The stabs of horror that strike when their toothless smiles become eternal sleeping grins, never to bubble, spit, or kiss your cheeks again.

But, alas! There is a pain greater than this! Just a hair deeper than the tragedy of a small child leaving this world. I should know, for I lived through it, though I was so sure

I would never survive it. It is when you lose him after you have already nursed him. Schooled him. Married him off to the prettiest girl in the village. When he dies the pain is earth-shattering. Shaking tremors born in the depths of the planet's ancient fault lines, creaking and throwing themselves about in protest of the ways of this world. The planet spinning out of control as it tries to understand how your child can be ripped from your arms, just to be placed in a box in the cold ground. The pain as wretched as losing a baby.

Basheer is the reason I lost my fear of dying. My handsome, singing boy.

The grandchildren were at our home on the afternoon that government demonstrations were concluding in the capital. The country was just a few weeks into its independence. A country that once seemed so sad could finally find a will to live on the promise of the right to rule ourselves. Gulam and I were watching Basheer's kids as we often did while their parents did their afternoon work. The youngest was just a few weeks old. We piled them into our vehicle, and Gulam and I set out to take them home when the sun began to set. It was a typical outing until people began to call out to us as we drove. "Mohamad! Stop! Stop! Stop!" Even this was in the realm of the expected. Someone needed help. Gulam was the driver of the town ambulance so people often called out to him on the road. "Ambulance Daddy" they called him. When we were stopped in emergencies, he never minded that he was off-duty, nor did I. We just did not know that this time, we were being stopped for our own sake. This was not just like any other call for help. We were being called to help ourselves.

From the first moment we heard it was Basheer, the

memories thereafter become crude. Fuzzy and unkempt like frayed ends of the white cloth that would later be wrapped around his body, as though this part of my memory refuses to recall. My body and consciousness rejected what was happening in those moments. My body became hot as my heart quickened, racing the way it had when I chased him around the house in his childhood. The *smack smack smack* of my slippers trailing along with me.

We would find out later at the hospital that he died on impact. Our running was futile as we raced to something that had already gone. His body flew into the air after being hit with such force. The driver was so drunk that he did not even believe he hit a man. When he was finally stopped a few streets further on, he was convinced he had hit a cow and not a man. His daughter implored from the backseat, "No, Daddy, you hit a person!"

But I did not retain any of these truths. I heard a chorus of voices shouting it, crying it, whispering it. "Shh, shh, nah say he dead, watch he mudda here." My husband felt the stillness of his artery when we got to the street on which he was lying. An examination that he did everyday on the job. Sorting out the dead from the living. But not tonight. Tonight he shared my fears and my denial of nature. Tonight we would rampage in search of the answer we so desperately sought. Tonight we would carry my dead son across the town and back again, all to seek news we knew we wouldn't receive. We prayed to God to give us what He had already decided to take. Our lives crumbling in minutes, and yet we relentlessly denied it. Like a couple quietly eating dinner inside a home that is up in flames.

We carried him into our vehicle and sent his children home with a relative. I still do not know if they could understand what they had just lost in that moment. The darkness of the night began to spread through the country. Unable to drive, Gulam sat with me in the backseat as his friend sped us to the hospital. The springs in the seat pushed up against my back and the old windows rattled with every bump and hole we clashed with on the way. Basheer's head was in my lap. My son asleep in my arms, blood leaving his body by the ounce every second. I held him close to my chest, frenzied at the sight of his blood, but willing myself not to scream. "Where is it coming from? We need to stop the blood! Apply pressure!" I implored all through our drive. My daughter had to use mugs in order to remove the remnants of his life from the backseat the next day. Blood, black and thick, piled up so high you would think every last drop left his body. The car became filled with dark red, and my clothes became drenched in his death. I held him the way I wanted to hold Gul and Roshan and the twins before they left me.

The light in the car flickered on and off. We shone flashlights in my boy's face to see if he was turning pale: the look of life draining from the body. In that long drive to the hospital we did all we could to avoid confronting what we knew was true, what we could plainly see with Gulam shining the flashlight into his eyes. Holding his head. Rubbing his fingers. Trying to massage life back into our son's body. Nudging him without shouting what we both wanted to shout. "Wake up! Wake up!" And there I sat, holding him in my arms the same way he was given to me when he was born. Cradling my baby on his first and last days.

We finally turned onto Parade Street and were in front of St. Joseph Mercy Hospital. Just a few lights were on in the building that was topped with a church steeple. The doctor ran to our car when he saw Gulam, the same man who brought him his patients each day. When the doctor's voice began to shake, I ran to the bathroom. I didn't want to be there to hear what I knew he would say. "Mr. Mohamad, your son is already gone." But Gulam would not believe it. He told the doctor goodbye, and I ran back to meet him at the car. He asked our driver to take us to the Public Hospital instead. We drove all the way to New Market Street, forcing what we had heard out of our minds. It was not right! What did that doctor know?! When the doctor at the Public Hospital ran up to the car, I ran to the bathroom again so I would not hear it. When I returned, Gulam's face looked older. The veins in his forehead were pronounced and his eyes were red, just like those of a woman I had once seen with burst blood vessels. He could not speak to me even though I was right in front of him. I saw his Adam's apple bouncing up and down, his throat working to choke back his agony and stifle the truth that we so skillfully avoided, until now. He never told me what the doctor said as I hid in the bathroom. But I knew he simply said, "He is gone already, Mr. Mohamad."

I did so well fleeing the news that I did not hear the actual words confirming our loss until a hearse pulled up in front of the hospital. A group of women were chatting nearby.

"Don't tell di lady! Don't tell di lady! She will die too if she hear her son dead!"

Oh, but I was already dead. Couldn't they see I was already dead?

■

His friends cried fiercely when the vehicle came for him. When the parlor men lifted his body, his arms and feet swayed lifelessly, like long blades of grass leaning and bending in the breeze. Much like the earth that he would be returned to in just one short day. It was a sight Gulam couldn't bear to watch as he wept and held Basheer's torso as they loaded him into the car.

I do not know how I got out of my clothes. How I washed the stains of blood from my skin, the same blood that runs through my own body, the blood I had given to him and he returned to me. I do not know how I arrived at my bed. But it was in that bed that I stayed. Bedridden for a time period that escapes me. I do not remember eating. But I remember sleep being the sweetest escape from the grief that commanded every ounce of my abilities. Voices fluttered about me. Male. Female. Young. Old.

"Jannah, try and come eat."

"Jannah, try and take some breeze."

"The children are here. Come and see, Jannah."

But I could not hear beyond the deafening sound of my heart breaking. I could only press my face into my pillow and wonder, "What kind of paradise is this?"

The Indo-Muslim Heritage of Guyana

The first Muslims in Guyana arrived in the African slave trade and belonged to the West African Mandingo and Fulani tribes. Islam was later reintroduced to Guyana in 1838 with the arrival of Indian indentured laborers. Despite the racial diversity of the religion's demographic, Muslims in Guyana are still referred to as "Fula," a term expressive of the link to the original Fulani roots of the country's Muslims and often used derogatorily by the country's Hindus and Christians. Of the Indians brought to Guyana between 1838 and 1917, only sixteen percent were Muslim while an overwhelming eighty-four percent were Hindu.[7] Existing immigration records indicate that the majority of the Muslims who arrived in Guyana and Suriname hailed from Uttar Pradesh, Lucknow, Agra, Fyzabad, Ghazipur, Rampur, Basti, and Sultanpur. Afghans, belonging to the Indian Pathan caste, were also among the indentured laborers and founded one of Guyana's oldest *masjids*: the Queenstown Jama Masjid, named after the original *masjid* that sits in New Delhi, India.

The customs of the Indian Muslims differ greatly, though not fundamentally, from those of Arab Muslims. This unique culture is academically categorized as Indo-Iranian, a realm of cultural expression that is closely tied to the Turkish camp language of Urdu and reminiscent of India's Mughal era. Urdu, with the rise of the Mughal Empire, became the principal language of Indian Muslims and remains today the official language of Pakistan and one of the official languages of India. Many Guyanese madrassas of the twentieth century taught Urdu in lieu of Arabic, not because of any deliberate cultural preferences, but rather because of the misinformation that had proliferated throughout the years conflating Urdu and Arabic as one and the same. These are common struggles of a diaspora reaching to remain connected with both their homeland and their inherited faith.

At the heart of Indo-Iranian heritage, literature and poetry functioned as valuable tools for the spread of Islam throughout South Asia. The era of the Mughals was a time flourishing with musical and poetic expression; quintessential illustrations of the Mughal era nearly always incorporate gatherings of people singing, dancing, and praising one another for their poetry and diction. As it was through these expressions of music, literature, and poetry that the Qur'an and the teachings of the Prophet Muhammad (peace be upon him) were able to flourish throughout the subcontinent, Indo-Guyanese Muslims similarly maintained their strong connection to music, literature, and poetry. *Qasidas*, Islamic devotional hymns, remain very popular in Islamic religious instruction in Guyana.

Prior to 1960, Muslim missionaries who visited Guyana were exclusively from India. It was not until after 1960 that Guyanese Muslims first made contact with the Arab world. Since then, with the advent of globalization and technological advancement, this contact has increased dramatically. The current development of Islamic scholarship as a whole is nearly exclusively rooted in the Arab world, primarily in Saudi Arabia. This scholarship is also limited to a handful of schools of *fiqh* (Islamic law), despite the original existence of dozens of schools of Islamic interpretation and thought. Because of this overwhelming Arab influence on current Islamic scholarship, the face of

Islam throughout the world has begun to become one of Arab homogeneity. As a result of this, in conjunction with the influx of Arab missionaries, the vibrant Indo-Iranian heritage has begun to be heavily challenged amongst Guyana's Muslims.

This phenomenon of Arabization has been placing Guyanese Muslims in direct contravention with their own heritage by imposing universally Arab manifestations of culture, packaged as necessary for proper adherence to religion. This imposition is one that calls for the severing of ties with many of the Indo-Iranian customs of artistic expression; it also linguistically prioritizes Arabic over Urdu, and refers to any practices outside of this narrow cultural sphere as *bi-dah* (evil innovations). Notably, a number of *maulanas* have visited various Muslim communities in the Caribbean and concluded that the musical and creative history of the Indo-Iranian Muslims are well within the parameters of Islam. This, however, has not prevented the challenges described.

This friction between Arab and Indo-Iranian traditions is a struggle that persists for Guyanese Muslims both domestically and in the diaspora. There is a deep struggle connected with the discarding of one's own cultural traditions, in this case due to a rising Arab supremacy that incorrectly proclaims to be the only cultural tradition consistent with Islam. Nonetheless, not all has been lost just yet with respect to Indo-Iranian culture and Guyana's Muslims. The development of Islamic scholarship, however, may lead to conclusions that require further dilution of these traditions, thus necessitating the need for a divergence from these divisive schools of thought, lest these traditions be lost altogether.

■ ■ ■

Leela

1979

I GREW UP ON THE EAST BANK OF THE DEMERARA RIVER, a pocket of the world rich in rice, cane sugar, and puritanical love. The roads are made of dirt that turns to mud, thick like pudding, during the rainy season, and cows roam freely on our highways and squat in front of government buildings. My home was a typical one for our area of town. You know, the poor part. Zinc sheet walls topped with a zinc sheet roof. When it rained it sounded like a hail of pebbles was cascading upon our heads, which was, surprisingly, soothing and serene for people who didn't have a choice anyway.

In the mornings, the voices of school children walking to the Diamond Primary School echoed off of our walls, making it impossible to sleep after seven. The boys always skipped in their black boots and dress pants with the front seam crisply ironed flat. The girls paced slowly in pleated skirts and white socks. Their hair glistening with coconut oil, neatly separated into two long and pristine braids, held together by bright red ribbons.

At an early age I told my mother I didn't want anything to do with those awful braids and miserable skirts. After putting up an unrelenting fight — and lying to the school headmaster about a burn on my leg — my mother finally quieted my bitching and got me approved to wear pants. I still had to wear my hair in a single long braid that my mother styled for me each morning, digging her powder pink comb with the twelve missing teeth into my scalp. "School dress code," they said.

My hate for skirts and ribbons and braids never raised any flags for my parents. I won't call them red flags because there is no element of alarm about who I am. Besides, what's wrong with red flags? The Hindus in this country quite literally plant red flags, tied upon tall chutes of bamboo as symbols of their religious work. The *jandhi* flags. I am sacred just the same. My parents were used to me running around in my brothers' hand-me-downs: large shorts and worn-out cricket jerseys were staples in my wardrobe. As a headstrong six-year-old who just really wanted to wear pants, even I didn't know that something was different. Until I knew.

Just two years into wearing pants to cover my ghost scar, I met Amritha. Her skin was milky brown like someone had added just a dash of ground nutmeg in the glass and swirled it around a bit. The same way my father made it when I had a fever or an ear ache. We sat three desks away from each other in our small classroom at the northern corner of the school, and I steadily sought and found reasons to walk over to the pencil sharpener on the counter near her seat, just so I could catch a glimpse.

We never talked about anything significant, if there is even such a thing as significant conversation for eight-year-olds. We just chatted about small things like earrings and coconut bread and worn-out school shoes. She never asked why I didn't wear skirts like the rest of them. It was normally the first thing that every girl at school asked me. But it was like she just understood without having to understand. A comfort like milk with nutmeg.

"Leela, how much do you need to sharpen your pencil?" my teacher shouted one day. "I'm telling your mudda to start sending you to school with proper supplies!"

And she did. She mailed her a letter, as I was famous for discarding the letters the school sent home with me by dumping them in brown water trenches on the way home. My mother beat me that night until her hands hurt. Each slap punctuated with single syllabic shouts.

"YOU — *slap* — GIVE — *slap* — THE — *slap* — TEACH — *slap* — ER — *slap* — TROUBLE?"

So I lost my fleeting counter-side chats with Amritha and had to think of new ways to be around her. I wasn't even sure that this was romantic love. But I did know that I never wanted to be friends with another girl so badly! And I knew that when I saw the brilliant movie posters that were plastered all over the city near the cinema house, I hardly ever noticed the hero, but always the beautiful heroines. Their thick-winged eyeliner, dainty nose rings, and long braids. The same braids that I didn't want on my own head. The same braids that I loved on Amritha.

The boys at school knew I was different. Some taunted me while others quickened their pace when I neared them, as though I was one of the rabid dogs that commonly roamed the streets. So I learned to treat them all like enemy combatants. I tripped random boys in the hallways and jeered them during lunch. They were all little assholes to me so I didn't care. They called me names and tried to hit me whenever I beat them in cricket. So I just hit the little shits back.

My parents became painfully aware of my vicious behavior

after a series of disciplinary measures taken by the school. There was just one kid, Wazir, whom my mom always told me to leave alone. Not that I ever wanted to mess with him; he never said anything mean, or anything at all, to me. "Aye gyal, you better leave that boy alone! He fadda just get knock down and dead!" Fine, ma. And I listened.

As I got older, the boys just made it too goddamned easy for me to access the girls. They practically handed them to me as though they did not want them. It wasn't until my teens that I realized I wasn't just obsessed with Amritha because I liked freakin' nutmeg milk. It was a timely revelation because the boys remained so blasted clueless. They desperately screamed for feminine attention by badgering the girls around them like their daddies did. Laughing at their skinny legs. Splashing fountain water at them during recess. Tying their long braids to the school benches when they weren't looking so that when they tried to get up, they'd be catapulted back down into their seats. They seriously risked fracturing necks for the sake of attention.

I'd thrashed a boy or two in my early teens just to save a girl or two from this savagery. As I got older and the boys grew stronger, I succumbed to biology and decided not to try to fight pound for pound and, instead, stuck to fighting the malnourished little boys. Once when I was sixteen, I punched a boy named Sunil for whipping this girl Sheena's legs with long, fine twigs as she walked to the minibus line-up. It was only after a hail of punches to my ribs that he realized I wasn't a boy. He retreated in the most sincere horror I'd ever seen — "Oh, shit!" By then my hair was styled in a bob and my large school shirt aptly covered the scarce breasts that I had.

Sheena and I made out behind the seawall that afternoon. Her mouth tasted like lime water and her neck smelled like Yardley's powder. When I unraveled her pigtailed braids, she had shiny ringlets of waves in her black hair that reminded me of the way dye disperses when dropped in a glass of water like we saw in chemistry class. The next day at school she refused to even look at me. A common theme that I would grow accustomed to over the years. Steamy love on one day, isolation on another. Even in adulthood, I remained surrounded by this cowardice, this uncertainty, this hurt. They were all spineless mollusks, satisfying their lustful libidos with me and then adorning themselves in red sarees and ancestral jewelry to marry the same men to whom I had given bloodied noses as a child.

"Leela, just let me marry you out to a boy from another village, and then you can do what you want," my mother would often plead. My existence caused my parents a lot of pain and embarrassment. People whispered when they saw mom and dad, half menacingly and half pitifully: *the poor parents of the lesbian girl.* You see, gay men were nothing new to this country. A gay man was called an "Aunty Man." At least that's how it's pronounced. People throw rocks at them as they walk the streets, and hetero men often beat them mercilessly if they feel they are uncomfortably close. It is an environment that breeds abundant and deep closets in which the nation's queers hide.

I was spared from similar displays of extreme repugnance for much of my life. I was too vile for even this kind of diseased and hateful recognition. I was still a woman. I was stuck in this nebulous box of femininity that was too delicate to abuse but too offensive to respect. I eventually turned to religion, much to my parents' delight, as a way of finding my footing in the grand scheme of creation. It was my one redeeming quality in their eyes. In a country filled with devoted hearts of all faiths, I too pained to know where I fit in with my maker.

I had to go beyond the beautiful temples to find where I belonged. I had to read on my own, pray on my own, and learn on my own. The *pandits* didn't tell us the truth about being gay and Hindu. To them it was a taboo that was rejected like a bad kidney. They belonged to a faith that truly welcomed me, yet remained faithful to a culture that shunned me. The devoted Hindus longed for a day when they could go to India on pilgrimage, but they never acknowledged that the most sacred of temples in Karnataka was dripping in relief sculptures of queer love. Love that maybe didn't even fit into neat boxes of categorization, but just existed organically in the same way that flowers bloom without regard for classification. They just exist.

The *pandit* in our village temple didn't teach me any of this. The books in the Golden Grove Library taught me that. The devoted never talked about Shiva bathing in the Yamuna River to become a woman and dance with Krishna. They didn't talk about the story of Arjuna's son, Arwan, in the Maharabharata epic: when it was decided that Arwan, still unwed, would be sacrificed for the sake of victory in battle, Krishna turned himself into a woman named Mohini and married him so that he could have a taste of romantic love before his death. Mohini even wailed like a proper widow for Arwan when he died!

Not a single religious leader taught me this. They did not lead me anywhere.

Whenever I sat in front of the prayer altar with vibrant magenta hibiscus flowers clasped in my hands, singing *bhajans* with my eyes closed in meditation, I knew that the congregation stared at me in disgust as though I was desecrating their sacred ground with my filthy reputation. Some of them knew I had already loved their daughters; some of them afraid that I would one day try.

■

One particular Sunday in temple, the rains were beating on the world causing the Demerara to overflow. The room was filled with both worshippers and passersby seeking refuge from the torrential rainfall. The sound of a woman babbling with her lady crew cut sharply through the sacred chants. Her voice crawled mischievously between my recitations and cracked the way my skin does in the dry season. "Is she here to worship the goddesses or to lust after them?" she proffered. She and her friends cackled wildly.

In truth she was lucky. I had reached a point of mystic peace in my adulthood. How lucky she was that I was so close to divine transformation, for it all rolled off of my chakra-aligned back. I had transformed from that young girl who would thrash all the boys in her path like an indiscriminate war criminal, to one who, in this moment, smirked sexily and thought to herself, "Why, yes, Aunty. I bring the 'gay' to the Gayatri mantra," and continued to recite the ancient verse, unbothered and unmoved.

> Om Bhuur-Bhuvah Svah
> Tat-Savitur-Varennyam
> Bhargo Devasya Dhiimahi
> Dhiyo Yo Nah Pracodayaat
>
> — The Rigveda

No matter how much they laughed or how many daggers they pelted at me with their mud brown eyes, I felt safer with these women than I did outside of the temple. We were all equally subjugated to the men outside of these walls: first to our fathers and then to our husbands. And yet this sisterhood had found yet another subjugation in which to place me. Didn't they see that we were in a common hell? That we were all stuck, so completely powerless, praying to the same Holy Mothers for comfort?

While we existed in the shadows at home, we sought light from Lakshmi's blessings. While we were forced into docility and silence outside, we built fortitude when we lay offerings at Kali's feet. We were so weak and Kali so strong: a gallant image of feminine destructive and creative power, her matted black hair flying wildly, her eyes enlarged in wonderment, her tongue extended in rage. Her face alone illustrated that she understood the pains of the women of the world. We prayed in our quiet circles of blighted womanhood with our eyes shut and our hearts screaming, like closed windows in the eye of a storm, imploring our grievances to The Mother Who Could Tear It All Up. Slaying the demons of evil in protection of her children. We were her babies and yet we held disdain for each other. She would surely destroy us next.

On the seventh night of Navratri prayers in 1979, I lost my sacred bubble. Of the nine nights, this was the night of worship for Kali Maa. It is a night of reflection on her strength and protection and gallantry. Yet the memory of this night inhibits me into weakness, with my body reduced into anxious tremors whenever I hear devotional bells shaking in piety or conch shells trumpeting in reverence. Even decades later I cannot withstand.

"Jai Maa Kali, Jai Maa Kali, Jai Maa Kali," I chanted as I placed my offerings at her feet. I gazed lovingly at the Dakshina form of The Mother, with one foot planted firmly on the ground, and the other on the chest of Shiva, indeed, destroying the Destroyer. I placed my offering near the far more threatening of the two feet. *Protect me, Maa.*

The temple was filled with smoke from the dense sticks, cones, and coals of incense, all breathing at once. My eyes watered in irritation and beads of sweat mottled my forehead and chest. It took me nearly fifteen minutes to move through merely ten feet of praying women to get to the exit of the foggy temple. The faithful were out in swarms, each with their own prayers and requests and appeals for The Mother.

When I emerged onto the dark street I exhaled in relief, my hands on my knees as I bent over to catch my breath. My off-white, cotton *salwar kameez* clung to my sweaty skin.

"Aye, girl! Leela!" I couldn't see who it was, but I knew it was coming from the throng of cars down the road where men normally sat and drank rum while their wives prayed in the temples to be saved from them.

"Leela!"

As I squinted my eyes and strained my sight, I saw that it was a very drunk Sunil walking toward me. The same Sunil I had started beating when he whipped Sheena's legs with twigs in high school. The same Sunil who backed away in horror when he realized I was a woman hiding in pants and hair styled like his own.

"Leela, you wearing *salwar* and ting now? Like you find ah man to fix you?" He was with two friends, and they guffawed in smug unison as they trailed behind me. The smell of drink pummeled off of their breath. I groaned in disgust.

"Like you know how fah fix your own wife?" I retorted quickly as I walked away.

"Fucking lady man!" he spat.

"Just leave me alone, Sunil!" I finally shouted. "Y'all already drunk and the prayers nah even done! Have some shame!"

I quickened my pace. Sunil's crew swiftly grew from a trio to a menacing group of six men. All of them were cussing, spitting at my feet, slurring and stumbling from too much of the golden rum. The sounds of the temple became more faint as I neared the dark street that would lead me to my home.

"Nasty bitch! Can't find no man to give she his bird!"

I halted and turned on my heel. I'd thrashed Sunil before, hadn't I? What use was it praying to The Mother if I could not emulate her? Ah, it was the night of Kali after all.

"Sunil, don't you ever so much as even watch in my direction!" I boomed as I walked right up to his wide face, covered in sweat and only visible from a bathing of moonlight.

My body shook as a sensation similar to a fever took over my skin. My chest erupted in pain as it collided with the rigid ground on the dark street. I brought my hands into fists, my nails digging into my palms, struggling to punch and strike. My arms were firmly constricted when I heard the sound of cotton ripping followed by the feel of open air on my bare legs. The marks of their fingers would remain imprinted just under my elbows for weeks.

I screamed until I bled from my throat. First Sunil, then another, and another, and another. Ripping and gnawing and penetrating, their sweat pooling at the base of my back while their callused hands pushed down on my neck and arms. My teeth remained clenched on the ground, biting down on the dirt as I shrieked. The veins on my arms protruded like the wires that I woke up the next morning to find connected to my wrists in the Public Hospital. The nurses whispered feverishly, but their eyes never met mine. Through my own dirt-filled shrieks I could still hear the *aarti* for Mother in its final verses. The conches blowing in noble chorus. The bells frantically clanging in fright. *Wake up, Maa! Wake up!*

And then, the world was still. The darkness released me from anguish. My body to be reanimated in the morning, with doctors and social workers half-heartedly working to make me whole. But part of me remained forever absent since then, that seventh night of the festival of the Goddess. Vanished into the comforts of blackness. Never daring to peek into the light again.

Guyana's Disposition on LGBT Rights

Guyana remains seemingly faithful to its lack of protection for the LGBT community. Same-sex relations is illegal as a matter of Guyanese law and is punishable by imprisonment for a term of two to ten years.[8] A male prostitute, prosecuted by the Georgetown Magistrate's Court in May of 2006, was fined $5,000 for "vagrancy and wearing female attire."[9] Cross-dressing was later found in a 2013 court decision to be legal, but not for "improper purposes." The court, however, failed to elaborate on what constitutes proper or improper purposes. As far as public life is concerned, it is still common for homosexuals, primarily gay men, to be violently and physically abused in response to public displays of affection.[10]

Although gay marriage is illegal, a wedding ceremony between two men took place in the capital city of Georgetown in March of 2004. After the ceremony, someone opened fire and shot one of the grooms in the chest, a story that remained headlined throughout the country for days.[11]

In October of 2015, the United Nations Committee

on Economic, Social and Cultural Rights (CESCR) urged Guyana to repeal their discriminatory laws against the country's LGBT community.[12] The Committee met with the Society Against Sexual Orientation Discrimination (SASOD), a national LGBT human rights organization, to discuss existing mechanisms for the protection of the LGBT community in schools, the work place, and government institutions. The result of the meeting was the grim conclusion that Guyana's LGBT community lacks even basic protections, thus denying them human rights that are well recognized by the international community.

SASOD provides services that aim to counter the lack of protection for the LGBT community. This is done through their reporting system, which allows people to report when they have been discriminated against because of their orientation, after which a SASOD staff member may assist them in seeking legal protections through other avenues. The organization conducts national campaigns for combating homophobia and promotes health awareness within the LGBT community. In addition to SASOD, the Guyana Human Rights Association (GHRA) supplements reformation efforts through legislative proposals and correspondence with United Nations committees.[13] Both organizations constantly work to repeal discriminatory Guyanese laws, but often with the result of little change.

■ ■ ■

Melissa

2010

"LIZ. I'VE BEEN THINKING. AND I MADE A DECISION."

"About what?"

"I'm ready to die. I've thought about it. And I'm ready. I know how I'll do it. I just...I just can't live without my dad anymore."

Within ten minutes she was in my living room. She ran from her house just one street away in her red and white flannel pajama pants and North Face snorkel that she'd had since we left high school two years ago.

"I'm hanging up and I'm coming over," she said. "Just give me a second."

I knew she wouldn't leave until she felt my mind was changed, my feelings calmed, and my safety assured. She was like this with me. All the time. Trying to guide my decisions like my mother. Yeah. That's right, she was certainly the mom in our friendship. I realized this three years into our friendship, at seventeen years old, when we cut our last class and ventured into a random tattoo parlor on Jamaica Avenue. The owner didn't even ask for IDs or give us a second glance. We just stood there staring at the menu of designs on the wall, bathed in the soft yellow light of the vintage lamps hanging above us.

We had this plan to both get something small. Something small, simple, and in plain black ink. That was the mantra. Those were the terms and conditions we worked out for our first tattoos. But, of course, Liz pussied out, and we ended up going to eat French fries with hot sauce at a nearby Chinese takeout spot instead. She still has no tattoos and never does anything risky. She only now started dying her hair because our grays have begun to sprout in displays of tragedy.

People always thought we were sisters. She's a little darker than I am, but our eyebrows arch the same way, and I guess that screams to unsophisticated onlookers: "Oh, they must have the same parents." But I suppose the way we behaved didn't really help to clarify the situation either. Once, when we were sixteen, we both got jobs as cashiers at this supermarket near our homes. I scanned three bundles of cilantro under the wrong inventory code and the customer's total came up to $238.52, for just the three bundles.

"Two hundred and thirty eight dollars!" the woman on the other side of the register cried.

"Yeah, man. Cilantro," I said, smiling with my eyes wide and unassuming like a dairy cow's. A swarm of profanities were, probably justly, hurled in my face while I corrected my mistake.

"Well, I guess that's why you're here. Too fucking stupid to finish high school, huh?"

And that set shit off. I repeat. That set shit off. We'd had our share of the racist Italian-Americans who would come in the store, speaking down to the Indians and the Hispanics working the cash registers. The management was no better. In fact, the store manager, a middle-aged Italian woman, outright refused to hire Black people. Everyone knew this. Even the store's Black patrons.

And despite all of our prior exposure to their special brand of prejudice, shit was set off. The lid was off the pot. The rubber met the road. Shit went down the day I overcharged for cilantro.

Liz stomped toward my register with her red cashier's smock coming loose in the back. The gel in her hair had turned white on some of the curls that sashayed behind her.

"WHO THE HELL DO YOU THINK YOU'RE TALKING TO? WHO?"

"This does NOT concern you!" the woman in front of my register replied. Her voice rancid like poison.

"Like hell it does! No one talks to MY sister like that! Wanna say that shit again? HUH?"

"Maybe you and your sister should have stayed in school and this wouldn't be the only job you can get."

"You are a racist piece of shit for assuming that we didn't finish school! Do you want to go outside?"

"You wanna go, we can go!"

"Well then, let's go!"

"HEY!" I roared. "If you touch my sister it will be over!!! Do not touch her!" The world was about to implode. Were we really about to fight this bitch?

The manager came. She apologized to the woman and made us take a break. The customer is always right, even when they're racist and hurtful and even when it took all of just thirty seconds to correct my mistake on the register. We were out of line. I mean, damn, yes we went off on that woman with all of our teen rage. The line was crossed miles ago. As young people still trying to figure out the right balance for dealing with assholes, this was on the Lose Our

Shit end of the spectrum. Now that we're both in our twenties and no longer angsty teens with passions as raging as our acne, we've found that the proper balance is lower volume, a slightly lighter sprinkling of the F-bomb, and a lot more wine to deal with the aggravation of having to choke down the very honest words that people deserve to hear.

After that day, we decided that we couldn't work together. At least not while we were in "customer service." I left the supermarket and went to work at Applebee's. It was better this way, better for the consumers of America that we not work together. A service to our countrymen. But in any case, it was plain to see why people thought we were actually sisters. We couldn't have been closer if we emerged from the same womb and suckled from the same breast. We would unleash upon random racist soccer moms for each other. We were so clearly each other's keeper.

A few months after our failed attempt on Jamaica Avenue, I got my first tattoo. It was small, simple, and in plain black ink. I etched a sleek *Om* with gray gradients into the skin behind my neck. And not in the ironic way like worldly White people with dreadlocks who do gap years in South Asia. More in the way of someone who has struggled with believing in God but somehow found her way back to temple on Sunday mornings. More in the way of someone who has aunts that pray over her to rid her of the evil eye, chanting in Sanskrit while burning her eyes with the smoke from their potent Five Roses incense sticks. In *that* way.

The *pandits* once told me that I was born between two bad moons. To make matters worse, I was not named properly. When a Hindu child is born the parents must consult with the *pandit* regarding an appropriate name based on the planets that would govern her life. In India, these names became your proper names. For us? It became our book names, and often, though not always, designated as our middle names. My parents gave me the book name Tanuja. They gave me an Anglo-as-hell first name and popped my book name in the middle name slot of my birth certificate. But I would find out years later that my book name was supposed to begin with a "Y" and not a "T". I didn't believe the *pandit* when he told me at fifteen that my life would be perennially difficult because of this.

"You were born between bad planets! When you were born, your father was not supposed to see you until your mother performed a special *puja*," the *pandit* explained. "Make sure to perform that *puja* before your father dies. Otherwise you will be unsuccessful throughout your entire life!"

He told me to fast—no meat—twice a week for twenty-one weeks. Liz is Muslim, but she still came with me and had the *pandit* advise her too. She fasted with me on my no-meat days. Even if she didn't believe in this stuff she wasn't messing around with no bad moons. She gladly ate chickpeas and corn along with me to cover her ass in case one of my two thousand deities decided to blight her for life. When I told my mom what the *pandit* said to me, she dismissed it as nonsense, much like everyone else I spoke to about it, even though I was kind of concerned. But I was young and I had a long window of time in which to perform the *puja* that would rectify the universe around me. After all, I just had to do it before dad died, right? Even my dad, the man who cared for and loved me the most in this world, did not think it was necessary.

Except I didn't have time. It only seems that way when you're too young to know better. Too young to care about how wrong we are about how much time we have left. My window shut. My bad planets have rotated in frenzy all about me ever since.

■

The summer before I turned eighteen, my fate was sealed. It was a still night in July. Too still. My dad wasn't in the house, so I went outside to check on him. The garage was dark and quiet, but I knew he went in there earlier. He often went in there to drink and listen to music and be alone with his thoughts. His car was still in the driveway. I grabbed a flashlight and went through the back door to the garage. I slid the square bar on the side of the flashlight upward to click it on. The light was white and harsh. I nudged the garage door open with my elbow and began searching with my narrow column of light. I was expecting him to be asleep. Instead, I saw the frame of his body midair. His head slumped to the side. His feet dangling just above the empty bottles that he'd consumed that evening.

I saw enough to send shrill shrieks throughout the block. When the police came, the night was a blur of sirens and tears and condolences. But my own screams just continued to echo in my ears. My bad planets locked into their inauspicious positions. My time was up.

I didn't tell Liz until the next morning. First, I sent her a text message. "I can't come to your party tonight. Sorry, girl."

As expected, my cell phone started ringing within a few minutes.

"Hey, girl. What's going on?" She asked. The tone of her voice told me that her eyebrows were knit together in concern.

"I can't come to your party today," I said firmly as I tried to keep my voice from devolving into hysteria.

"What? Why? What happened?"

"My dad died." I began to sob uncontrollably while keeping my phone up to my ear with my right shoulder as I held the long handle of the kitchen broom at an angle to get under the cupboards in the kitchen. Soon the relatives would be over. Their shoes would be in piles by the door. Soon the *pandit* would be over. Soon the house would be filled with sacred chants for prayers to properly send my dad into his next incarnation.

"Oh my God!" she shrieked. "I'm coming now, bye!"

She was there in minutes. I could tell that she had just jumped out of her bed, still wearing her glossy red basketball shorts and a gray vest with rubber slippers; her hair half clipped, half flying away. I'm not even sure that she brushed her teeth. As soon as I saw her I cried. She hugged me and wept. I half-hugged her back without letting go of the broom. Soon they would be there. I had to keep cleaning. I had to clean and make tea and prepare snacks. This was a wake house now.

And so the funeral came. And it went. We cremated my father and conducted prayers the requisite thirteen days after he was put to rest and again one year later. My mom, my two brothers, and I struggled each day following that night in July when he left us in the garage. I never completed the *puja* to save me from failure in this life.

We all tried so hard to make sense of what happened. Of how it happened. Of how things like this happen. Why was this the way he chose? To suspend himself from the garage ceiling? What would become of my bad planets now?

We kept our house but tried moving away for a while to get away from the scene of where my dad murdered himself. We got a condo out on Far Rockaway and left the house in Ozone Park empty. All of us too afraid to go back. Liz came once to our place out on Far Rockaway. She took a train and a bus and then walked the rest of the way. When she came we made *channa* and ate it while watching MTV even though the curry powder wasn't fried properly and hung on the individual chickpeas in clots like boogers. But I ate it because I knew how desperately she wanted me to feel full. My family and I eventually returned home to Ozone Park. The commute to school and work was unreasonable from the Rockaways, and the cost was too high. It just wasn't our home. So, we went back to face our demons. The very demons that nearly killed me.

■

Some time around my nineteenth birthday, two years after my dad left, I called her and told her.

"I'm hanging up and I'm coming over," she said. "Just give me a second."

We sat on my bed when she arrived, and she told me what I knew she would tell me.

"You have too much to live for. You need to speak to a therapist. What can I do? How long have you felt like this? I cannot allow this. What will your little brother do without you? Melissa, what about ME?! What am I supposed to do if you die?"

We talked until the early hours of the morning, sitting cross-legged on my bed. I told her I felt better. That speaking to her really, really helped. That I would go for counseling like she suggested. I'm not sure that any of that was true but by the way her eyes glazed and she planted herself on my bed, I knew I needed to say something to ensure her that I would live through the night.

We never talked about that night again. And I never brought it up to her again. When we saw each other we just escaped into absurd movies. Trying to forget the world that had brought us here. These were our Bollywood nights. These films are absolutely sensational and ridiculous. Bizarre things happen that audiences just don't question despite sometimes being either too outlandish or even regressive. It became our new thing. It's still our thing. Watching prototypical outrageous Hindi films while guzzling our weight in white wine. A sweet escape for people like me trying to escape inauspicious fates and bad moons.

■

Things Twenty-Somethings Talk About When Watching Hindi Films While Drunk:

- Do you think Shah Rukh Khan cheats on his wife?
- Since when is Priyanka woke?
- You're about to get married, walking down the aisle, when Hrithik Roshan says he wants to marry you and take you to live in his Goa bungalow. What do you do?!
- Isn't Hrithik, like, forty?
- What kind of wine is this?
- Shahid Kapoor. Just in general.
- Kaho Naa Pyaar Hai versus Jab We Met for best Hindi film ever debate.
- Ew, skip this song the words don't even rhyme.
- What kind of wine is this?
- How do we find a guy like this? Let's go to India and find a guy like this.
- Yo, that back up dancer looks like your ex.
- What kind of wine is this?

And so on. We may, admittedly, have had these conversations even while sober. For the most part, this was life. These were our chemically induced weekends with a sprinkling of club nights and hot dates that we would rush home to talk about with each other as soon as they were over.

"Dude tried to do me in his car when he dropped me home, Liz!"

"Oh my God what did you do?"

"I said I had to go because my dog was barking."

And we'd collapse in laughter after every story.

Somehow, in some way, the pain became manageable. Even the pain of knowing that my dad never left us a goodbye or a reason. When the cops came to the house, they searched the garage for a note. It was one of the first things they looked for, as their training tells them to do. But none of us could find one. We couldn't find a single explanation. An answer. A reason. What was it about this life that made him leave us to live it without him? While he was busy caring for us and cooking for us and raising us, why didn't he take the time to attend to his own wellbeing? Oh, the lingering questions, the lack of reason; they burn through my consciousness, poisoning any happy thoughts that may so rarely dance across my mind. Piercing any guises of peace that I may so temporarily enjoy. The lack of reason holds me by my shoulders and stares deep into my large, brown eyes. Angry. Demanding to be looked at. But I cannot find an answer. There are no answers. Just deafening silence.

The silence remains permanently etched in my brain, much like the series of tattoos that I would accumulate over the years permanently marks my flesh. Flowers, tribal art, my dad's signature, an anagram that reads both my mom's and my dad's names depending which way you look at it. After getting each one, Liz would implore, "Okay, Melissa, no more tattoos after this one!" And then we'd end up in Forever 21 one day trying on dresses, and I'd take off my shirt to unintentionally reveal to her that I hadn't listened to a word she said. "What's that? When did you get THAT?!"

I don't know the exact day, or what I was doing or feeling, when I stopped feeling like I had to join my dad. One day I just accepted his decision and didn't allow it to mean that it had to be my own. I stopped researching on Google the easiest ways to commit suicide. I stopped drinking as much as I used to. I stopped feeling like I had to leave this world in order to be with him in the next. I found meaning in the world I was in. When I was forced to grab the reigns of the household — paying bills, cooking dinner, raising my little brother — I had to put myself second to everything I wanted. Even death. I came second to the mortgage and my family and my elephantine responsibilities. And yet it is in this chaos that I reaffirmed my will to live; that I realized that death was not the way to join him, for I join him everyday.

He is in the air I breathe and in the sun that bathes my skin when I step out to work in the morning. He is in the woman who smiles at me as I walk to the deli for a sandwich. His face continues to live on mine.

■

"Are you sure you're gonna be okay?" Liz asked as she put her shoes back on. Still stressed. Less manic.

"I'm gonna be fine. Just text me when you get home," I said.

"I'll call you."

"Fine."

And she ran home with her pajamas fluttering in the gusting

winter wind. Her hood pulled over head. She called when she got home, as promised, but seemed afraid to say goodbye. So, we slept on the phone together. Our breathing synchronized in phone static. Our cellphone batteries were dead by morning.

The Phenomenon of Guyanese Suicide

Guyana has the highest rate of suicide in the world, a phenomenon that, to date, no one has been able to aptly explain. While deep poverty, alcohol abuse, and easy access to deadly substances provide the perfect cocktail for a suicide hotbed, Guyana's 44.2 suicides per 100,000 people per year, as reported by the World Health Organization, begs for a greater explanation than the described elemental breakdown.[14] To worsen the issue, there is a deficiency of psychiatrists in the entire country as well as a shortage of psychologists and social workers. This lack of resources has allowed the Guyanese people, a population in desperate need of clinical care, to spiral into a seemingly unmanageable state of depression. To make matters even worse, Guyanese are typically stigmatized for mental illness, and deaths in such cases are categorized as inauspicious or inspired by dark spirits. Stigmatization prevails throughout the Caribbean and is the result of a clear lack of discussion on a public level. Accordingly,

Guyanese both at home and in the diaspora continue to take their lives at alarming rates.

The leading method of suicide in Guyana has been the ingestion of pesticides, which is readily available to many farmers living in the country's rural areas. As the Guyanese government has historically done very little to address these tough issues related to mental health, many people have turned to religious leaders for guidance in navigating the arduous waters of mental illness. This, however, is largely ineffective, as religious counseling often postures depression and other mental illnesses as ailments that can be cured by prayer or a more firm belief in God. The Guyana Foundation, a private philanthropic organization, has recently started initiatives to tackle suicide at a grassroots level. Thus far, it has conducted training throughout the country for religious leaders and health workers alike. It has also spearheaded campaigns to educate communities throughout the country about misconceptions about suicide and mental illness by working with national media outlets.

Despite these efforts and the newfound international recognition that Guyana has gained in connection with this issue, there are still no emergency services available for Guyanese who are thinking of ending their lives.

■ ■ ■

Takuiba

1980

IF YOU ANGER THE SPIRITS OF THE STREAMS, THEY MIGHT overflow in rebellion. The river will slither into our huts like the python that almost strangled Papa, softening our mud walls until we have to move again to new grounds. More downstream, always. I try my best to be mindful of the spirits because I really want to stay on this new ground we have taken as our home. There are so many trees with low branches for climbing, and Big Sister and I get more time to play games because the gathering lands are close enough to the hut that Mama lets me meet her there.

When Big Sister got her belly she couldn't talk to anyone. She was so ill that the other tribespeople thought that *Kanaima* had possessed her and was turning her into a chicken. Once, the evil *Kanaima* entered an elderly woman, and she removed the innards of her grandchild with a blade before finally killing herself. When Big Sister stopped talking, the tribespeople thought Papa was being punished for killing the young boy from the Carib tribe who once tried to enter our grounds at night.

Papa is the chief of our village and very well respected amongst our people, the Arawak Kapon. The war leaders say he is the greatest chief they'd ever had, even though Arawak have not warred in many, many years. It was only a few days after I was born, thirteen years ago, when the Carib boy came into our enclave upstream of the Mazaruni. At that time, the people living on the coast started bringing more and more metal equipment to our grounds, forcing us, each year, to retreat further and further downstream. Papa said that the tribe's leader at that time sent a letter to the President asking about the future of the pipe project and informing him that the Arawak must live upstream as per our tradition. When *Makunaima* created our tribe, he placed us at the top of the Mazaruni. It would surely anger him to see how much lower we had fallen. But, alas, each year since my birth we have had to move to new grounds, the metal pipes uprooting our earth from north to south. Soon, we will be completely downstream, or away from the river altogether, despite where we were divinely placed.

Some people say that the boy who intruded our village was not a Carib, but was from the outside town. They speculate that he wore denim and not the identifying fringed cloth of the Carib, plus his hair was cut in neat lines. After Papa stabbed him in the fright of the night, our tribe's shaman traveled for three days to visit Papa and warned him that his next child would be doomed. The spirits would avenge the life that Papa had taken outside of war.

But when Little Sister was born Mama said it was her easiest birth yet. And everyone finally dismissed the prophecy as the blabbering of an aged shaman. Little Sister is the fattest of us all. She has the biggest appetite and the healthiest flush of red to her cheeks. We were certain that the spirits had decided to spare us their anger. Until Big Sister became ill. Big Sister lost her voice before we knew she was pregnant. She stopped speaking, stopped eating, and stopped smiling. When Big Sister's belly became big, the color drained from her face and the glowy part of her eyes became orange like the fireflies that flutter around the *blim blim* trees.

I begged *Makunaima* to save her from the demons! I fasted for three days, and I danced with Little Sister along the Mazaruni until my feet blistered and my head swayed in hunger. The Ancient One answered and saved her, but after she gave birth, she announced that she would not be bearing anymore children. Papa became angry with her but was relieved that she survived. Had her illness not improved, the War Leaders would have been forced to slice the unborn child from her stomach in order to combat the omen that was following their Chief. Papa said no woman has ever survived a purge like this.

Just before my thirteenth year, I got my blood. Mama gave me gleaming shell earrings and a beautiful necklace made of bones. Big Sister didn't speak with me much for the first few days that followed. She was the first person I showed when I felt the moistening on my cloth. She told me not to tell Mama. She said that she would wash my old cloths and have Little Sister bring me new ones; that I just had to retreat to the stream during the day and return to my bed before Mama came back from gathering cassavas. She begged me to stay silent.

But I had to tell Mama. My stomach pained so badly, I thought the spirits were punishing me for some forgotten sin. When I told her, Mama smiled and kissed my face all over. She cooked me a salty broth before I went to sleep. I shared it with Little Sister who was sulking in the corner, suddenly unhappy with her plain cassavas. Big Sister fed her son at her breast as I drank my broth. Her voice left her again for three days.

It took eight days for my bleeding to stop, and I quickly wished it had never begun. I tried to return the earrings and bone bib to Mama, but she giggled and said it couldn't be undone. That once it came, it was as much mine as my shadow.

"What *Makunaima* sends down from the sky cannot again live amongst the clouds."

I spent every day washing and drying my small blood cloth. Little Sister did not have time to help me in her busy days of play and gathering with Mama. On the fourth day, Big Sister finally spoke and told me about the paper cloths that some of the Arawak who live closer to the coastal people use. She said that they threw them out by burning them after each use and that the women did not attend the church when they bled. These Arawak did business with the town people and sometimes wore denim pants and collared shirts because the miners were offended by scant loincloths. In the exchange of business, the coastal Arawak got many things, including large black tanks of water and papers for when women bleed.

Every day Mama asked me if I stopped bleeding yet. She checked my groin to be sure. She said that, each month, it would get better and I would become so accustomed to it that I would forget it was there, like the birthmark on my shoulder. When the bleeding finally stopped she hugged me very tightly before scolding me for forgetting to wear my bone bib and earrings.

"You are a woman now. Big Sister has not removed her jewelry, and you shall not go a day without yours." She set the necklace around my neck and clasped the ends together in a secure knot. The bones were cold against my chest.

Two days after my blood stopped, just before high noon, Papa called me from outside the hut.

"Takuiba, did you know that the Arawak Kapon were divinely placed upstream of the Mazaruni? That *Makunaima* created our tribe to dwell there eminently?"

"Yes, Papa," I replied.

"Poor one, your whole life you have known nothing but this downstream existence. The metal projects have robbed you of proper devotion for The Ancient One."

"I still dance toward upstream during the fast, Papa," I countered. "Surely *Makunaima* can still see us here. Are his eyes so small?"

"How would you like to see the upper Mazaruni?" he asked.

"To see it?"

"Yes, do you want to see where our people were created?"

"I would love to!" I said excitedly.

"I will take you tomorrow in the Chief boat. Just before high noon, like now."

"Okay, Papa," I confirmed. I ran back to the hut and squealed in excitement to Big Sister.

She lost her voice again.

■

The next morning, just before high noon, I raced to the stream to meet Papa by the Chief boat. I became worried that he'd left without me as I'd slept later than usual. I tossed and turned in elation all night. I couldn't wait to see new grounds. Mama, Big Sister, and Little Sister left at sunrise to gather the harvest. I'd been spared from work because of my planned trip with Papa.

When I got to the stream, Papa was already in the boat

checking the floor for cracks and cleaning the dirt off of the outside bark. I sat inside and waited quietly until he finally began to row. We didn't speak for the entire journey, which lasted until nightfall. The travel was peaceful. The waves of the river were cooperative, almost tame for this time of year. I thought to myself that maybe *Makanaima* was making it easy for us to return to our rightful home upstream by calming these famously unsteady waters. When we finally stopped, I was asleep on the cross-plank in the rear of the boat.

"We're here, Takuiba. Wake up."

Papa's voice was thunderous in the deafening silence of the night. I could barely see the new grounds: the moon was obstructed by intruding clouds and we had no fire just yet.

Papa left me by the stream while he went to gather sturdy leaves for our sleeping mats. When he returned he handed the leaves to me to assemble while he built a small fire. I was too tired to eat, but Papa found a rodent and scorched him for a quick skewered meal. I fell fast asleep before he finished consuming it. The warmth from the flames coated my skin in a sweet lullaby. I dozed off in a comfort that made me feel like these upstream grounds really were our rightful home. I never enjoyed such quick sleep in our own hut.

The fire had dwindled to a humble hum when Papa's hand touched my waist. The softening flames were the first thing I saw when my eyes shot open. My loincloth had been securely knotted to withstand the long journey, but it had somehow come undone on both sides. He placed his hands on my shoulders and turned me on my stomach. I felt his rough hand reach below and pull my cloth out from underneath me. What happened next I didn't recognize. I fainted from the pain that shot up through my spine as he pushed his hips feverishly in hurried flourishes. It was as though *Kanaima* had begun his evil journey through my body. The spirits took possession of my body, leaving my old self behind like snake skin shed at the top of the Mazaruni River. Never to be worn again. When I awoke from my faint the fire had completely died out. I could see the pink dawn crawling to peek above the trees of this land that *Makanaima* made just for us. This land that I was told belonged to me.

■

By the time we returned home the next day, it was nightfall again. Our entire voyage back was silent. Papa was at the head of the boat rowing skillfully to dodge the more hostile waters we encountered on our return. Retribution for the ease of our travel the day before. When we pulled up to the shore, the tribespeople were there to greet us. They carried fire sticks and arranged large embers in rows to provide light for the spectacle of our arrival.

Mama met me at the boat and took my hand to help me out, as though she knew that I would have trouble balancing myself. When my feet were planted on the ground she held me closely and whispered in my ear.

"You have done your duty for our clan and for our tribe. You and Big Sister will be among the most respected by the Great Spirits."

Little Sister ran to the shore and pulled me by my right arm to see the sandals she stitched by herself the day before. I kept my eyes fixed on Mama, even as Little Sister pulled me further and further away. Energetically seeking my validation for her work, Little Sister asked me to wear the sandals she so proudly cut and stitched without Mama's help. She grew frustrated with every question that went unanswered by me, every statement that went unacknowledged. Through the hut door I could see Big Sister nursing her son by the light of a small fire that she often kept kindled near her bed. She looked at me silently and knowingly, all at once, as I walked into the hut. We both lost our voices for days.

The Amerindians (Indigenous Peoples) of Guyana

Guyana's native peoples, known as the Amerindians, still largely remain true to their tribal heritage in the country's interior. While many tribes have modernized by adapting the country's school system as their own and by implementing mechanical enhancements such as plumbing and electricity, some remain faithful to the original ways of the first tribespeople. The main Amerindian tribes of Guyana are the Arawak and the Carib, the latter being the more powerful, and the tribe that gave the Caribbean its name.

The Arawak is a group of indigenous peoples scattered throughout South America and the Caribbean who speak related Arawakan languages. Many Arawak today still speak the native Arawak language of Lokono, in addition to English, French, Spanish, or Dutch, depending on the country in which they live.[15] The term "Arawak" comes from the tribe's own language, meaning "cassava root," their main crop food. They were reputed as the "best humored Indians of America" by European explorers (Major John Scott, 1665) vis-à-vis neighboring tribes that, through an exceedingly Western lens, were historically described as being extremely hostile and prone to war. Today, the Arawak live in Guyana, French Guiana, Suriname, Trinidad, and coastal areas of northern Venezuela. Only a few thousand Arawak remain in the world today.

Each Arawak community is led by its own local leader; centralized government was never a characteristic of the tribe throughout its history. These local leaders are known as the chiefs of the individual communities. Traditionally, the Arawak living in the interior dwelled in thatched huts and commuted by way of dug-out canoes. They are, historically, a farming people, and their main harvest, as already mentioned, includes potatoes and cassava. Aside from their far-reaching reputation for being good-natured people per European standards, the Arawak were also famed for their pottery and woodcarvings.

The Carib, on the other hand, were the most powerful and numerous of the indigenous peoples in Guyanese history. Also referred to as the Kalinas, the Carib were known as the warriors of the Amerindians and settled along the Mazaruni River, the Essequibo River, the Pomeroon River, and the upper Cuyuni River in Guyana. Early European explorers claimed to have witnessed cannibalism in Carib tribes, thus the word "cannibalism" derives from a distortion of the name "Carib."[16] Although once a thriving tribe, the arrival of European settlers resulted in great loss of life for the

Carib through both warfare and disease, a common narrative in the stories of native peoples throughout the world. With respect to diet, the Carib consumed high volumes of protein obtained from iguanas, ducks, and myriad species of fish. Much like the Arawak, they steered away from centralized government and still maintain systems of local leaders consisting of chiefs and war leaders. Today, the Carib are largely settled along the shores of the rivers of Guyana, as well as in Venezuela, Suriname, French Guiana, and Brazil.

The Carib and the Arawak share a common ancient spiritual system based on the worship of nature, ancestral spirits, and a variety of gods; both tribes utilize shamans and other metaphysical designations to cure illnesses. The smoking of tobacco also plays a large role in the religious rituals of both tribes. Furthermore, both tribes subscribe to highly patriarchal social frameworks. Arawak and Carib women alike are generally assigned the roles of gathering food, cooking, and caring for children, while Arawak and Carib men are generally responsible for hunting and protecting the women and children from warring tribes.

In 2000, the Human Rights Committee of the United Nations released a report detailing the grave injustices and threats to existence faced by the Amerindian peoples of Guyana. Not only do these indigenous people lack equality before Guyanese law but their tribal homes are also consistently threatened by mining and logging,[17] as the Guyanese government regularly demarcates Amerindian lands for various economic activities. As a matter of further complication, when Guyana became one of the largest drug exporting countries in the world, many smugglers and dealers utilized the interior jungles, where many Amerindians live, for the transport of cocaine and marijuana, leaving the Amerindians at a very difficult and violent geographic crossroads.

Over time, more and more Amerindians have begun to leave the interior jungles to settle in the towns and villages of Guyana, thus inciting worries regarding the loss of native languages and traditions. Many Amerindians work in government positions and have fully acclimated to life outside of the interior, even with respect to embracing popular religions. Nonetheless, the Amerindians in Guyanese society continue to face great discrimination, which is largely based on ignorance and misinformation regarding their intelligence and/or prejudice regarding the ways of life of the country's native people, which is often characterized as backward or immoral. Despite this repulsion, the Amerindians of Guyana, both the Arawak and the Carib, have left an everlasting stamp on Guyanese cultural identity, as traditional Amerindian cuisine, pottery, woodcarvings, and leather goods continue to serve as identifying components of Guyanese heritage.

■ ■ ■

Genevieve

2016

YOU'VE GOT TO RUN UNTIL YOU TASTE BLOOD IN YOUR mouth. Your chest tightens. It feels like a rubber band ready to snap, and then you taste it: the iron rust on your tongue that lets you know you will survive. Run until you've no ability to distinguish between your feet and the uneven concrete. Until your body merges with the floor. The *clank clank clank* of the chains echo behind you, telling you there is no time to be tired. You must run home even though the chains that reach for your ankles tell you that this is not home. They are chasing you in the same way your white blood cells would attack an infection. You are a foreign specimen. A threat to their health. They want to cut you out the same way cancer cells will be cut from your thyroid years later. They want to oust you from their sweet parish of whiteness. So you run.

The steps feel all too familiar. Like you'd been running since you were a child. You vaguely remember one night in the old country when you dozed on your thin bed made of sponge, only to be awoken by your mother's shrieks. You were surprised to find yourself propped on her hip hours later, just feet away from plummeting to a watery death. Running. Fleeing from evil before you could even develop a moral compass to know what evil is. Running is how you live. You did it in your sleep.

Your mother ran. She ran from the old country and left you with your grandmother. Your grandmother ran the rum shop and raised you with kisses and slaps. She was a strict father and loving mother, all at once. What choice did she have when your father was too busy drinking and your mother was busy running? Seven years later your mother would finally send for you. You'd take your first plane ride to JFK Airport and find that you had a whole new life waiting for you where the streets were made of concrete and not the sand-dirt mixture that always got between your toes when you walked to the market. You had a whole new life in Queens, where your mother bought her own home and your neighbors were as white as your new iron fence.

In this new place your mother was no longer a teacher, even though she often recounted to you how hard she worked to become one in the old country. Now, she would wake up before the sun to put on black slacks and assorted blouses and sit in a cubicle for eight hours entering figures into a database. A job that would lead her to need two surgeries for carpal tunnel. And even this was worth it.

In this new place the teachers couldn't beat you like the ones at home. You remember the one time your teacher slammed your head into your desk in your small, village schoolhouse, causing your ear to bleed as your earring became dislodged. You remember your grandfather, your grandmother's brother, running to the schoolhouse to thrash your teacher for touching you. You remember never being hit again. But, here, in this new home, the teachers couldn't touch you regardless of Grandfadda's threats. But the classmates you wanted to make your friends would chase you home with long, swinging chains, threatening to kill you if you didn't leave their pristine community alone. Who would save you now?

And so you have to learn to start running. Each day after school. You run, your feet pounding on the concrete of what is supposed to be your retreat. This is supposed to be where you were running to. But running does not stop. Asylum never reached. For now there are new evils that rear their heads. Evils that no one could imagine in the old country. You start saying phrases like "back home" to refer to your old village because it has become clear that this new home is anything but that. This is simply the place to which you ran. The chains and slurs slicing at your back, each day worried that this is the day you will not be fast enough. Your little feet will not propel you far enough in enough time.

Your mother gets tired of the running. Tired of your feigning illnesses to avoid going to classes where you must sit with the same people who plot your torture. So she sells the house in Wakefield, the one she so proudly purchased as an edifice of the end of her running, and you move to a part of Queens where you learn more people like you have been moving as well. The more people like you move in, the more the people the color of your fence move out, exclaiming that the "quality of the neighborhood has gone down!" They run so fast you can see smoke coming out of their rears. They cannot bear the smells of your food or the intonations of your accent.

Everyone says you can stop running now, but you cannot ever believe it. Who are they to say that you should stop doing the very thing you've been doing since before you could walk? Did you not watch your mother run each time the radio blared and you heard your father singing on the other end? Begging her to accept his apologies?

Did you not run to the trench with your mother where she had planned for you both to drown? Did you not see your mother run from the old country, leaving you there for years while she devised a way to stop fleeing? Did you not learn that you must run anyway? Had this not become the way you'd survived? What does one do when they are not running? What do we do with our feet now?

You love your new home, your take-two at this new life. You love this home where the antibodies just clear the hell out when you come in, as no one bothers to attack you as a disease anymore. You paint your new fence black and get zoned for a school where there are throngs of students who share your surname. You learn this on report card day when the administration sets up a separate line for the school's Singhs. So you join the line proudly and make small talk with the others in queue. Asking where "back home" is for each of them. Howling in excitement when, by chance, you meet someone from your own little hamlet of the old country. Confused to meet Sikhs who share your namesake but look at you as though you are an alien they have never encountered.

You meet your husband in this new home. Your eyes meet at a nightclub that plays the melodies of the old country while stocking the liquors of the new. He loves your voluminous hair, kinked with curls, and the hips you inherited from the grandmother who raised you. So you start yet another new home with this man and trade in your prided "Singh" for the momentous "Mohamad" and delight in no longer having to collide your feet with the ground to survive. You relax. You recline. You untangle your tired muscles and your wary grief. You breathe.

Breathe! they instructed you each time you were in labor. First for your daughter, who left your womb nearly two months early, and later for your son, who came two days late and snored during his delivery. *Breathe!* you had to remind yourself when the urge to run took over your body when Lizzie came home one Tuesday from Kindergarten to tell you that her classmate said they couldn't be friends because they weren't the same skin color. You had to breathe and find a way to stay.

You transitioned from a life of trying to escape to a life of trying to remain planted, unmoving like the metaphorical tree your grandmother would sing about in her favorite Church hymn.

Just like a tree that's planted by the water,
Lord, I shall not be moved!

And it is in this state of newfound permanence that your daughter climbs into bed with you one night. Now an adult, her body revealing the same hips that you delighted in at her age, but that she weeps over as she learns that the trending clothing doesn't fit her just the way it's supposed to. She snuggles next to you, her skin warm, but dry because she always forgets to rub lotion on her skin after the hot showers she enjoys so much. "Mommy," her voice quivers, "I feel like I can't stop running."

Richmond Hill, New York

In 2014, an article started making its way, rampantly, throughout my social media platforms. Dozens of my cultural peers eagerly shared a *Washington Post* article written by a man who had recently "discovered" our small New York neighborhood. The author explained that he had never even heard of Little Guyana before his "discovery." In the very first sentence he swiftly oversimplified Indo-Guyanese existence as looking "Indian but sound[ing] like Bob Marley when they speak,"[18] even though Guyanese and Jamaican accents are markedly different.

I can understand that my peers were excited to finally receive recognition on a platform so large. But I could not dismiss the condescension that was so very clear in his impromptu trip to my home. The home that the women before me labored to find. As the fifth largest immigrant group in New York, the Guyanese population is largely concentrated in Richmond Hill, Queens, where many Guyanese immigrants began to settle in the late 1970s. Prior to the arrival of these immigrants, Richmond Hill was mainly populated by European families (Italian, Dutch, British, Irish, Scottish, Danish, and German).[19] The new migration wasn't well received by the original residents. Rather, a displacement took place whereby as the new Guyanese population steadily came in, many of the European families steadily showed themselves out. In the meantime, this process of displacement was peppered with experiences of intolerance toward the earliest Guyanese immigrants.

Those who moved into Richmond Hill in those early days often recount difficult experiences with respect to acceptance and assimilation. It is with great deference that I tip my hat to those trailblazers who established a sense of community and culture that my generation can now enjoy, an accomplishment that they labored for without much recognition in the end.

There is not much formal documentation of this small enclave of Queens that can only be described as enchanting and strange all at once — all the trappings of what it is like to return home. The central and famed Liberty Avenue is lined with roti shops, saree shops, and jewelry shops. In the cold months, it comes alive on the weekends when everyone comes out to buy their greens and spices while older women shout, "What ah pound for this!" over a long line of patrons. In the warmer months, its pulse becomes more lasting. The music gets louder; soca, reggae, and Hindi tunes all making special appearances from passing vehicles and homes alike. Snow cone, coconut water, and mango vendors all compete for your attention. People pretend not to notice that someone is slicing a coconut with a machete openly in the street. It can be a lot to take in for those who are unaccustomed.

It is as close to being "back home" as our parents can muster and as close to being planted in our heritage as first-generation American kids, like myself, can ever hope to have. And it is with great gratitude that I acknowledge those who have carved out this delicate comfort for me and my kin. I will forever be ashamed of the years we spent despising it, talking down on it as a place for "FOBs" or the uncultured, boasting that we would rather hang out in "the city." With adulthood comes appreciation for the struggles of those who made it possible for us to exist comfortably without fear of running. Thank you for making me a home I cannot wait to return to, no matter where I am in the world. I am happy to run home to you.

■ ■ ■

Elizabeth

2017

TRAUMA IS PERSISTENT. TRAUMA IS UNIQUE. TRAUMA IS encompassing. Trauma is inherited. Trauma finds life in the cries of all the women before you. All of their pains and abuses still alive in your veins. Pumping through the wary chambers of your heart, coexisting with the very systems that give you life. All of your identities wilt in defeat.

Trauma is knowing that your maternal grandpa physically abused your grandma until she no longer wanted to live. It is crying when you think of the happier, safer days she cannot now enjoy because her dementia keeps her stuck in the time of her pain long ago. Trauma is knowing that your dad grew up without his father, so you're wracked with guilt every time you argue with him. As though you are being ungrateful for the boon of having him in front of you—breathing, living, and loving. It is learning that your paternal great-grandmother had her first child at fifteen, and it comes back to you when your parents lock you in your house all summer for speaking to a boy at fourteen.

Trauma is accepting the damage that poverty inflicted upon the life of your maternal great-grandmother — a single mother who persevered in a life of unconvention. Trauma is holding your best friend as she sobs at her father's funeral. It is attempting to slowly reconstruct who she used to be for each day thereafter — small brushstrokes in painting a masterpiece you have watched crumble and slowly re-emerge. Trauma is learning of a girl who was gang raped in the streets of the old country while half of the village pretended to be asleep, and the other half was too consumed in prayer. It is learning that this was the punishment deemed necessary for the perceived deviancy of her orientation. Of who and how she chose to love. Trauma is learning about an Amerindian chief who raped his daughter per unchecked customs that reign just a few miles away from a sprawling coastline country with its own assortment of unchecked customs. A country where people hang themselves, drink poison, and engulf themselves in flames at a rate that surpasses all other countries in the world per capita. Trauma is the internalization of others' pain. All of their sorrows colliding with yours until you can no longer tell whose losses belong to whom.

Trauma is when your body started to change and everyone around you began treating you differently. Like the way you were growing was indecent and improper. It is when you receive clear instructions to carry yourself impeccably, for as a new lady, you were no longer just "Lizzie." You were now, at large, Wazir's Daughter. A title that made you the representative of his legacy, all reduced down to your modesty and palatable femininity. Trauma begins in your first fight with your father and comes back in your first fight with your husband. It pervades generationally and episodically, sometimes dimming, but always aflame. Sitting in the core of your gut like nasty bile that steadily creeps into your throat and comes out as words you never meant to say.

Trauma is being told not to bring shame to the family, so you carry the weight of that duty on your young, weak back. All of their secrets weighing on your spine. You wince in pain for the pressure of untold feelings constricted in your chest. Trauma is struggling to discern your identity in a world that is obsessed with truth and confirmation. It is learning that, for you, no such confirmation exists, as you descend from a lowly and historically forgettable rung of Indian society. From slaves performing physical and sexual labor for white men. You descend from those the world has long deemed as insignificant.

Trauma is being told not to speak too loudly or too much or too deliberately or too *anything*, as it wasn't becoming of a good lady. So you stay in your room and write in journals that would forever live under the shadows of your bed. The trauma exorcised from your body and onto the pages. The trauma became less traumatic as you scribbled swiftly across narrowly lined pages.

■

When I first started writing it was because I was angry. I was eight years old and had just been introduced to the wonders of Hindi cinema. Each week my dad brought home VHS tapes with simple labels indicating the title, headlined actors, and subtitles provided for the film. Between films I analyzed the pages of my mom's childhood scrapbook. Every page was covered with images of old-time Bollywood actors and actresses with brief interruptions for newspaper clippings related to

Princess Diana or Bruce Springsteen. I was consumed with Hindi cinema in a way that surpassed my previous obsession with the Spice Girls. With every film I began to develop a sense of cultural connectedness that Baby Spice could never give me with her tongue dripping in the melody of the Queen's English. I began to position myself with confidence on the complicated spectrum of my heritage and history: part Indian, part Chinese, part African. There was that one grandmother who bore a child for her Scottish overseer, but the family never factored him into our legacy even though he continued to haunt us every time a baby was born with his eyes. "Count me in," he whispers menacingly from his colonial grave. These movies helped me begin to understand myself for the first time in my life. They allowed me to recognize that I belong to a heritage beyond what I have been allowed to fathom. They allowed me to start the process of my homecoming.

After my first dozen films I became disenchanted nonetheless. Each one was the same! Each one was more or less faithful to the same assortment of storylines:

- Boy and girl fall in love but they are not the same caste. Higher caste family complicates.
- Boy and girl fall in love but they are not of the same social status. Richer family complicates.
- Boy and girl fall in love but one of them is already arranged to marry someone else. The arranging family complicates.
- Boy and girl fall in love but they are not the same religion. Both families complicate.
- Boy and girl fall in love, but boy's evil clone fudges up the whole romance. Original and clone complicate.

- Boy and girl fall in love but they do not end up together. They pick up their romance in their next incarnation. Their reincarnated identities complicate.

I jotted down my thoughts about this on my Lisa Frank stationary and then rewrote them neatly on wide-ruled loose leaf. "These films are like chocolate. I love them. But if I have too many, I'll get tired of them." I lied and listed that I was thirteen years old, as that was how old you had to be to have your words printed in the monthly publication to which I was sending my comment. I took many stamps, to be safe, from my dad's computer desk drawer and sent off my letter to the Mumbai address provided on the last page of the magazine. Thank goodness for that second grade lesson on how to properly mail a letter to Santa Claus.

The following month I went with my dad to the movie rental store on Liberty Avenue in Queens. I asked him to buy me a copy of *Stardust* magazine, and he did. No fuss. Dad was like that when I asked nicely. On the way home I carefully searched each page of the magazine as I sat in the backseat of the car until, alas! I found my comment. Printed! *Submitted by Elizabeth Mohamad, 13.*

I smiled stupidly the entire ride home and kept opening to the page to see it again and again. My dad eyed me suspiciously in glances through the rearview mirror. When I got home, I sheepishly presented my mom with the comment that was printed in a magazine that she had been reading since her teens. She gleamed and giggled and called my dad over to the kitchen to see it. "No, no! That's not part of the plan, lady!" I thought to myself. I was terrified of what my dad would think, or worse, say (scream). I lied about my age.

This clearly suggested that I was focusing more on these films than I was on my schoolwork. I was already on my dad's bad side for my failure to memorize my multiplication tables that week.

"But the teacher only wants us to learn up to the ten times table!" I would cry. "Why are you making me learn the twelve times table?"

"I look like your teacher?" my father roared. "I don't know what kind of teacher you have. You will learn up to thirteen by Sunday, you just watch!" I only learned up to ten.

His reaction to my *Stardust* publication floored me. It turned out that he was elated. He smiled so widely that his eyes nearly closed as his face could hardly contain his grin. The first sign of crow's feet made an appearance along the edges of his eyes. It was the same expression he had when he was recalling old stories with old friends. Like his anatomy could not contain his joy. It was like he didn't even see that I lied about my age!

That day writing became my lifelong loophole. Whenever I was silenced by my duties of femininity, writing became the medium through which my voice could boom thunderously on paper. I could argue contentious issues, cackle like a villain, or cry the tears I never wanted anyone to see. It became the vanquisher of my trauma.

■

In spite of my parents affording me a very comfortable life, the pains of the memories they tried to shield me from still hurt me deeply. This made my obstacles seem larger than they were, because I attached these larger pains to my own experiences, spiraling into grief unnecessarily, for the traumatized had already survived. It became known in my family that I was one who felt everything so deeply. Not in moderate emotional bouts. Once, I even had an epiphany about my mortality after a low-speed fender bender. My heart has only ever known the language of intensity.

And so I grieved. I grieved for not having been born a boy, so that I could acknowledge the opposite sex without discipline and scorn. I grieved over the way my dad laughed with my brothers when they spoke to girls on the phone, while I felt like filth because a male classmate instant messaged me. I grieved for not being able to sit around the table and discuss politics, while men, guzzling the famed Guyanese "liquid gold" of El Dorado rum, did so freely over card games and dominoes. I grieved for being told to be quiet, when all I wanted to do was express. When my opinions came from men's mouths, they were celebrated by the people around me. When they came out of my own mouth, it was branded as too extreme or too confrontational to ooze off of the tongue of a girl.

As I grew from girlhood to womanhood, I idolized the women who gained seats at the table I so desperately wanted to join. The women with unruly hair, who cussed and smoked cigarettes while intellectually battering the elitist men who sat beside them. The women who passionately discussed politics and didn't find shame in admitting that they didn't even know how to fry an egg or prepare *dhal*. They intimidated the men they encountered because they dared to establish a whole new system of valuation for themselves. They were a beacon of light in the darkness that I felt was constricting me.

Writing was my freedom. It allowed me to become the woman I'd always dreamed of becoming. As I grew and lived in a world that was increasingly volatile and peppered with anti-Muslim sentiment, I quickly learned that the dark experiences of my ancestors were not the only burdens I would carry with me. This life would give me darkness of my very own. I would become so encased in darkness that it would ultimately lead me to take my husband's name after marriage solely because the beauty of the beloved Prophet's name was too dubious for many of my countrymen — mainly the ones I met in classrooms and interview rooms. As a Mohamad, I was the problematic Muslim girl. As a Jaikaran, I became the token Indian girl. Both made me ill. But at least one afforded me some humanity. Surely, simply existing as a Muslim has been the largest source of my own interactions with trauma.

From childhood to adulthood, the only representations of Muslims I was ever exposed to in mainstream popular culture were what I understand today as outright demonizations. This is the only world I have ever known. This world where Muslims are devotedly painted with the most evil brushes known. Even now as I pen these words I wonder: when was the last time I saw a film that didn't use the *adhan* as the background audio for a sinister scene on terror? When was the last time a Muslim character was relevant outside of the context of warfare? Finding writing meant creating my own representation — for myself and for my spiritual tribe. It meant joining a community with other writers who were struggling to represent themselves as well. We found freedom in each other.

Writing also saved my cultural kin from generations of inherited trauma, as we articulated all of the issues and questions we had been suppressing all these years. It saved my dad from the limitations of cultural rules that told him his only daughter was supposed to be docile, obedient, and unthreatening. I have finally accepted this truth: that reading my thoughts on paper is less offensive than hearing them come out of my mouth. My dad learned to respect my contrarian personality through my pen. My writing is how he came to value my voice. It is how he has been able to love me more completely.

When I started law school at twenty-three, he reached the peak of his pride. It was unimaginable to me that the same man who told me to "sit properly" and "speak delicately" would be the same man hootin' and hollerin' for me to pursue a career where I am paid to argue. Out loud.

Except now I can't. I struggle. Every single day.

I can argue with my parents and my brothers easily. I can throw attitude at my cousins and laugh uninhibitedly with my husband. This is all no problem. But in finding writing, I have misplaced my physical voice when I need it the most. While my hand can firmly hold a pen and write my thoughts coherently and deliberately, my voice still shakes to articulate these very words aloud. It constricts in remembrance of my name, of my color, of my descent from the insignificant. Restricted by the muscle memory of both my inherited and lived trauma. Before a judge, before a professor, before a crowd of faces that don't look like mine. In circumstances that feel unfamiliar, in spaces that lack the safety of my home, I feel like running away.

I have evolved into a woman with convictions that I uphold even when heavily tested. Yet my voice remains unchanged. Apologizing unnecessarily and stumbling over my words.

"Yes, your honor, my apologies."

"No, professor, I'm sorry, what I meant to say was this."

"I'm sorry, maybe I'm not understanding this fully, but I'd like to suggest something."

Just avoid conflict lest you be deemed too confrontational. Lace your words with deprecation. Apologize when all you want to do is be bold. Smile when all you want to do is scream. My voice booms when I tote my pen. But my voice box? My voice box needs to be reminded every day that I deserve to be here.

■

Trauma flirts with your sanity in unlikely places. Like an inappropriate suitor who asks for your number at a funeral. It reminds you of its significance in your most peaceful moments. Like just as you're recounting a good day before bed, only to have your mind drift to all the horrors that generations of women have borne for the sake of your comfort. Truly, I do not fear the day when I will be questioned by the Creator. But I fear my reunion with my foremothers and the questions they will ask me. "Why have you lost your language, child?" "Have you made the most of the life we gifted to you with our blood?" I do not have worthy answers.

Trauma breeds insecurity. Foaming at the brim when greeted with complacency. Growing into impenetrable dragons breathing fire into your delicate, grieving chest.

Annihilating trauma requires the annihilation of your inhibitions. It requires accepting that it is there, wriggling clumsily through your flesh, and that it is just as much a part of you as your blood type or favorite song. Over time, it becomes a scattering of sorrowful footnotes worthy of reverence in the pages of a longer book of redemption. Destroying trauma means loving your identity. It means decolonizing the way you understand yourself. It means forcing yourself to speak and falling in love with your voice. It manifests when you proudly converse in the broken English of the old country. When you force yourself to speak before crowds and shed the discomforts of your old self. When you wake up each morning and tell yourself that you are deserving. When you stop obsessing over the regressive things that your culture told you to care about, like the darkness of your complexion or the widening of your hips. So you spend the day outside of the shade and in the sun, and when you dance you shake your hips with abandon in celebration of the anatomy some very powerful women made for you from scratch. The women who speak to you at night through dreams that make it hard to concentrate the next day. It manifests when you choose for yourself a lover who would never dream of telling you to sit right or speak softly, who leads you in prayer and invites you to sit at the table you'd always wanted to join, with liquid gold in hand.

To the women who braved untold pains before I came into this world: thank you for my redemption. I thank you, but I will never forgive your abusers for all of the generations of inherited trauma that now swims in thick, syrupy streams through my veins.

You have all freed me in ways I have only begun to understand.

■ ■ ■

Glossary

Adhan: the Muslim call to prayer

Bahu: daughter-in-law

Bhajan: Hindu devotional hymn

Bharaat: groom's wedding procession

Boujie: sister-in-law, specifically your brother's wife

Chadr: woman's head cover

Changpao: traditional Chinese dress; long jacket/tunic

Channa: chick peas

Dhal: Indian purée made of either split peas or lentils

Fiqh: body of Islamic law

Imam: the person who leads prayers in a mosque

Jandhi: Hindu prayer service

Jannazah: Islamic funeral sermon

Kanaima: an evil spirit that possesses people and causes them to commit murder, according to Indigenous religions of South America and the Caribbean

Makunaima: the God of Creation, according to Indigenous religions of South America and the Caribbean

Masjid: Muslim house of worship; Arabic for mosque

Nikkah: Muslim wedding ceremony

Om: a scared syllable that occurs at the beginning of most Sanskrit mantras

Pandit: a Hindu scholar, sometimes also a practicing priest

Puja: act of worship in Hinduism

Qasida: Islamic devotional hymn

Salwar kameez: women's attire of trousers fitted around the ankle, can be tight or loose, accompanied by a tunic and scarf

Sources

Domestic Violence in Guyana

1. "Domestic violence still widespread in Guyana-US State Dept. 2015 Report." *Kaietuer News*. April 21, 2016. <http://www.kaieteurnewsonline.com/2016/04/21/domestic-violence-still-widespread-in-guyana-us-state-dept-2015-report>
2. <http://www.ngocaribbean.org/index.php/cascadia-protocol-guyana>
3. "Survey shows Guyanese generally accept Domestic Violence." *Kaieteur News*. March 9, 2015. <http://www.kaieteurnewsonline.com/2015/03/09/survey-shows-guyanese-generally-accept-domestic-violence>
4. <http://www.hands.org.gy/files/dvguyana.pdf>

A Brief History of African Slavery in Guyana

5. "Slavery on the Plantation." <http://www.guyana.org/features/guyanastory/chapter26.html>

The Indo-Caribbean

6. Jaikaran, Elizabeth. "The Indo-Caribbean Experience." *Brown Girl Magazine*. December 1, 2015. Republished by *The Huffington Post*. <http://www.browngirlmagazine.com/2015/12/the-indo-caribbean-experience-now-and-then>

The Indo-Muslim Heritage of Guyana

7. Chickrie, Raymond. "Muslims in Guyana." 2001. <http://www.guyana.org/features/guyanese_muslim.html>

Guyana's Disposition on LGBT Rights

8. "Guyana: Treatment of homosexuals and state protection available to them (2004 - September 2006)." Immigration and Refugee Board of Canada. October 20, 2006. <http://www.refworld.org/docid/46fb72f9a.html>
9. "Male Prostitute Fined for Vagrancy, Female Attire." *Stabroek News*. May 16, 2006.
10. Johnson, Ruel. "The Fear of Stones; HIV/AIDS and Homophobia in Guyana." *Guyana Chronicle*. May 31, 2006.
11. "Shooting at Gay Wedding in Guyana Injures One." *The Advocate*. March 31, 2004. <http://www.advocate.com/news/2004/03/31/shooting-gay-wedding-guyana-injures-one-11877>
12. "UN Committee Urges Guyana to Repeal Discriminatory Laws." October 26, 2015. Society Against Sexual Orientation Discrimination (SASOD). <http://www.sasod.org.gy/sasod-blog-un-committee-urges-guyana-repeal-discriminatory-laws>
13. "Responses to Information Requests — Guyana: Treatment of homosexuals and state protection available to them (2004 - September 2006)." Immigration and Refugee Board of Canada. October. 20, 2006. <http://www.justice.gov/sites/default/files/eoir/legacy/2014/02/04/GUY101803.FE.pdf>

The Phenomenon of Guyanese Suicide

14. Mohammed, Farahnaz. "Guyana: mental illness, witchcraft, and the highest suicide rate in the world." *The Guardian.* June 3, 2015. <http://www.theguardian.com/global-development-professionals-network/2015/jun/03/guyana-mental-illness-witchcraft-and-the-highest-suicide-rate-in-the-world>

The Amerindians (Indigenous Peoples) of Guyana

15. "Main Amerindian Groups up to the Nineteenth Century." <http://www.guyana.org/features/guyanastory/chapter3.html>
16. Rouse, Irving. *The Tainos.* Yale University Press: 1992.
17. "Concluding Observations of the Human Rights Committee: Guyana." United Nations Human Rights Committee (UNHRC). April 25, 2000. (CCPR/C/79/Add.121)

Richmond Hill, New York

18. Cavanaugh, Ray. "Little Guyana, An Indo-Guyanese Enclave in Queens." *The Washington Post.* October 9, 2014. <https://www.washingtonpost.com/lifestyle/travel/2014/10/02/38ec1260-4998-11e4-a046-120a8a855cca_story.html>
19. "South Richmond Hill Neighborhood Profile (2011)." Queens Economic Development Corporation. <http://www.queensny.org/qedc/neighborhoods/economy/reports_profiles/Richmond_Hill_Neighborhood_Profile_ed.pdf>

About the Author

Photograph: A. S. Nagpal

ELIZABETH JAIKARAN was born in Brooklyn, raised in Queens, and currently resides on Long Island with her husband. She graduated from the CUNY City College of New York in 2012 and from New York University School of Law in 2016. She has written for numerous platforms, most prevalently for *Brown Girl Magazine*, and has published along a spectrum of genres, from legal analysis to comedy.

As an author and a lawyer, Jaikaran hopes to be a voice for communities residing in underrepresented margins. She is the proud child of Guyanese immigrants.

9 781941 830420

CPSIA information can be obtained
at www.ICGtesting.com
Printed in the USA
FSHW011505301218
54487FS